DEVIL'S FORD

BRET HARTE

1st WORLD
LIBRARY
Literary Society

Devil's Ford

Bret Harte

© 1st World Library, 2007
PO Box 2211
Fairfield, IA 52556
www.1stworldlibrary.com
First Edition

LCCN: 2007934084

Softcover ISBN: 978-1-4218-9622-9
Hardcover ISBN: 978-1-4218-9722-6
eBook ISBN: 978-1-4218-9522-2

Purchase *"Devil's Ford"*
as a traditional bound book at:
www.1stWorldLibrary.com/purchase.asp?ISBN=978-1-4218-9622-9

1st World Library is a literary, educational organization
dedicated to:

- Creating a free internet library of downloadable ebooks

- Hosting writing competitions and offering book publishing
  scholarships.

1st World Library Literary Society

Giving Back to the World

"If you want to work on the core problem, it's early school literacy."

- James Barksdale, former CEO of Netscape

"No skill is more crucial to the future of a child, or to a democratic and prosperous society, than literacy."

- Los Angeles Times

"Literacy... means far more than learning how to read and write... The aim is to transmit... knowledge and promote social participation."

- UNESCO

"Literacy is not a luxury, it is a right and a responsibility. If our world is to meet the challenges of the twenty-first century we must harness the energy and creativity of all our citizens."

- President Bill Clinton

"Parents should be encouraged to read to their children, and teachers should be equipped with all available techniques for teaching literacy, so the varying needs and capacities of individual kids can be taken into account."

- Hugh Mackay

CHAPTER I

It was a season of unequalled prosperity in Devil's Ford. The half a dozen cabins scattered along the banks of the North Fork, as if by some overflow of that capricious river, had become augmented during a week of fierce excitement by twenty or thirty others, that were huddled together on the narrow gorge of Devil's Spur, or cast up on its steep sides. So sudden and violent had been the change of fortune, that the dwellers in the older cabins had not had time to change with it, but still kept their old habits, customs, and even their old clothes. The flour pan in which their daily bread was mixed stood on the rude table side by side with the "prospecting pans," half full of gold washed up from their morning's work; the front windows of the newer tenements looked upon the one single thoroughfare, but the back door opened upon the uncleared wilderness, still haunted by the misshapen bulk of bear or the nightly gliding of catamount.

Neither had success as yet affected their boyish simplicity and the frankness of old frontier habits; they played with their new-found riches with the naive delight of children, and rehearsed their glowing future with the importance and triviality of school-boys.

"I've bin kalklatin'," said Dick Mattingly, leaning on his long-handled shovel with lazy gravity, "that when I go to

Rome this winter, I'll get one o' them marble sharps to chisel me a statoo o' some kind to set up on the spot where we made our big strike. Suthin' to remember it by, you know."

"What kind o' statoo—Washington or Webster?" asked one of the Kearney brothers, without looking up from his work.

"No—I reckon one o' them fancy groups—one o' them Latin goddesses that Fairfax is always gassin' about, sorter leadin', directin' and bossin' us where to dig."

"You'd make a healthy-lookin' figger in a group," responded Kearney, critically regarding an enormous patch in Mattingly's trousers. "Why don't you have a fountain instead?"

"Where'll you get the water?" demanded the first speaker, in return. "You know there ain't enough in the North Fork to do a week's washing for the camp—to say nothin' of its color."

"Leave that to me," said Kearney, with self-possession. "When I've built that there reservoir on Devil's Spur, and bring the water over the ridge from Union Ditch, there'll be enough to spare for that."

"Better mix it up, I reckon—have suthin' half statoo, half fountain," interposed the elder Mattingly, better known as "Maryland Joe," "and set it up afore the Town Hall and Free Library I'm kalklatin' to give. Do THAT, and you can count on me."

After some further discussion, it was gravely settled that Kearney should furnish water brought from the Union Ditch, twenty miles away, at a cost of two hundred thousand dollars, to feed a memorial fountain erected by Mattingly, worth a hundred thousand dollars, as a crowning finish to public buildings contributed by Maryland Joe, to the extent

Bret Harte

of half a million more. The disposition of these vast sums by gentlemen wearing patched breeches awakened no sense of the ludicrous, nor did any doubt, reservation, or contingency enter into the plans of the charming enthusiasts themselves. The foundation of their airy castles lay already before them in the strip of rich alluvium on the river bank, where the North Fork, sharply curving round the base of Devil's Spur, had for centuries swept the detritus of gulch and canyon. They had barely crossed the threshold of this treasure-house, to find themselves rich men; what possibilities of affluence might be theirs when they had fully exploited their possessions? So confident were they of that ultimate prospect, that the wealth already thus obtained was religiously expended in engines and machinery for the boring of wells and the conveyance of that precious water which the exhausted river had long since ceased to yield. It seemed as if the gold they had taken out was by some ironical compensation gradually making its way back to the soil again through ditch and flume and reservoir.

Such was the position of affairs at Devil's Ford on the 13th of August, 1860. It was noon of a hot day. Whatever movement there was in the stifling air was seen rather than felt in a tremulous, quivering, upward-moving dust along the flank of the mountain, through which the spires of the pines were faintly visible. There was no water in the bared and burning bars of the river to reflect the vertical sun, but under its direct rays one or two tinned roofs and corrugated zinc cabins struck fire, a few canvas tents became dazzling to the eye, and the white wooded corral of the stage office and hotel insupportable. For two hours no one ventured in the glare of the open, or even to cross the narrow, unshadowed street, whose dull red dust seemed to glow between the lines of straggling houses. The heated shells of these green unseasoned tenements gave out a pungent odor of scorching wood and resin. The usual hurried, feverish toil in the claim was suspended; the pick and shovel were left sticking in the richest "pay gravel;" the toiling millionaires themselves, ragged, dirty, and perspiring, lay panting under the nearest shade, where the pipes went out listlessly, and conversation sank to monosyllables.

"There's Fairfax," said Dick Mattingly, at last, with a lazy effort. His face was turned to the hillside, where a man had just emerged from the woods, and was halting irresolutely before the glaring expanse of upheaved gravel and glistening boulders that stretched between him and the shaded group. "He's going to make a break for it," he added, as the stranger, throwing his linen coat over his head, suddenly started into an Indian trot through the pelting sunbeams toward them. This strange act was perfectly understood by the group, who knew that in that intensely dry heat the danger of exposure was lessened by active exercise and the profuse perspiration that followed it. In another moment the stranger had reached their side, dripping as if rained upon, mopping his damp curls and handsome bearded face with his linen coat, as he threw himself pantingly on the ground.

"I struck out over here first, boys, to give you a little warning," he said, as soon as he had gained breath. "That engineer will be down here to take charge as soon as the six o'clock stage comes in. He's an oldish chap, has got a family of two daughters, and—I—am—d—d if he is not bringing them down here with him."

"Oh, go long!" exclaimed the five men in one voice, raising themselves on their hands and elbows, and glaring at the speaker.

"Fact, boys! Soon as I found it out I just waltzed into that Jew shop at the Crossing and bought up all the clothes that would be likely to suit you fellows, before anybody else got

Bret Harte

a show. I reckon I cleared out the shop. The duds are a little mixed in style, but I reckon they're clean and whole, and a man might face a lady in 'em. I left them round at the old Buckeye Spring, where they're handy without attracting attention. You boys can go there for a general wash-up, rig yourselves up without saying anything, and then meander back careless and easy in your store clothes, just as the stage is coming in, sabe?"

"Why didn't you let us know earlier?" asked Mattingly aggrievedly; "you've been back here at least an hour."

"I've been getting some place ready for THEM," returned the new-comer. "We might have managed to put the man some-where, if he'd been alone, but these women want family accommodation. There was nothing left for me to do but to buy up Thompson's saloon."

"No?" interrupted his audience, half in incredulity, half in protestation.

"Fact! You boys will have to take your drinks under canvas again, I reckon! But I made Thompson let those gold-framed mirrors that used to stand behind the bar go into the bargain, and they sort of furnish the room. You know the saloon is one of them patent houses you can take to pieces, and I've been reckoning you boys will have to pitch in and help me to take the whole shanty over to the laurel bushes, and put it up agin Kearney's cabin."

"What's all that?" said the younger Kearney, with an odd mingling of astonishment and bashful gratification.

"Yes, I reckon yours is the cleanest house, because it's the newest, so you'll just step out and let us knock in one o' the gables, and clap it on to the saloon, and make ONE house of it, don't you see? There'll be two rooms, one for the girls and the other for the old man."

The astonishment and bewilderment of the party had gradually given way to a boyish and impatient interest.

"Hadn't we better do the job at once?" suggested Dick Mattingly.

"Or throw ourselves into those new clothes, so as to be ready," added the younger Kearney, looking down at his ragged trousers. "I say, Fairfax, what are the girls like, eh?"

All the others had been dying to ask the question, yet one and all laughed at the conscious manner and blushing cheek of the questioner.

"You'll find out quick enough," returned Fairfax, whose curt carelessness did not, however, prevent a slight increase of color on his own cheek. "We'd better get that job off our hands before doing anything else. So, if you're ready, boys, we'll just waltz down to Thompson's and pack up the shanty. He's out of it by this time, I reckon. You might as well be perspiring to some purpose over there as gaspin' under this tree. We won't go back to work this afternoon, but knock off now, and call it half a day. Come! Hump yourselves, gentlemen. Are you ready? One, two, three, and away!"

In another instant the tree was deserted; the figures of the five millionaires of Devil's Ford, crossing the fierce glare of the open space, with boyish alacrity, glistened in the sunlight, and then disappeared in the nearest fringe of thickets.

Bret Harte

CHAPTER II

Six hours later, when the shadow of Devil's Spur had crossed the river, and spread a slight coolness over the flat beyond, the Pioneer coach, leaving the summit, began also to bathe its heated bulk in the long shadows of the descent. Conspicuous among the dusty passengers, the two pretty and youthful faces of the daughters of Philip Carr, mining superintendent and engineer, looked from the windows with no little anxiety towards their future home in the straggling settlement below, that occasionally came in view at the turns of the long zigzagging road. A slight look of comical disappointment passed between them as they gazed upon the sterile flat, dotted with unsightly excrescences that stood equally for cabins or mounds of stone and gravel. It was so feeble and inconsistent a culmination to the beautiful scenery they had passed through, so hopeless and imbecile a conclusion to the preparation of that long picturesque journey, with its glimpses of sylvan and pastoral glades and canyons, that, as the coach swept down the last incline, and the remorseless monotony of the dead level spread out before them, furrowed by ditches and indented by pits, under cover of shielding their cheeks from the impalpable dust that rose beneath the plunging wheels, they buried their faces in their handkerchiefs, to hide a few half-hysterical tears. Happily, their father, completely absorbed in a practical, scientific, and approving contemplation of the topography and material resources of the scene of his future labors, had no time to notice their defection. It was not until the stage drew up before a rambling tenement bearing the inscription, "Hotel and Stage Office," that he became fully aware of it.

"We can't stop HERE, papa," said Christie Carr decidedly, with a shake of her pretty head. "You can't expect that."

Mr. Carr looked up at the building; it was half grocery, half saloon. Whatever other accommodations it contained must have been hidden in the rear, as the flat roof above was almost level with the raftered ceiling of the shop.

"Certainly," he replied hurriedly; "we'll see to that in a moment. I dare say it's all right. I told Fairfax we were coming. Somebody ought to be here."

"But they're not," said Jessie Carr indignantly; "and the few that were here scampered off like rabbits to their burrows as soon as they saw us get down."

It was true. The little group of loungers before the building had suddenly disappeared. There was the flash of a red shirt vanishing in an adjacent doorway; the fading apparition of a pair of high boots and blue overalls in another; the abrupt withdrawal of a curly blond head from a sashless window over the way. Even the saloon was deserted, although a back door in the dim recess seemed to creak mysteriously. The stage-coach, with the other passengers, had already rattled away.

"I certainly think Fairfax understood that I—" began Mr. Carr.

He was interrupted by the pressure of Christie's fingers on his arm and a subdued exclamation from Jessie, who was staring down the street.

"What are they?" she whispered in her sister's ear. "Nigger minstrels, a circus, or what?"

The five millionaires of Devil's Ford had just turned the corner of the straggling street, and were approaching in single file. One glance was sufficient to show that they had already availed themselves of the new clothing bought by Fairfax, had washed, and one or two had shaved. But the result was startling.

Through some fortunate coincidence in size, Dick Mattingly was the only one who had achieved an entire new suit. But it was of funereal black cloth, and although relieved at one extremity by a pair of high riding boots, in which his too short trousers were tucked, and at the other by a tall white hat, and cravat of aggressive yellow, the effect was depressing. In agreeable contrast, his brother, Maryland Joe, was attired in a thin fawn-colored summer overcoat, lightly worn open, so as to show the unstarched bosom of a white embroidered shirt, and a pair of nankeen trousers and pumps.

The Kearney brothers had divided a suit between them, the elder wearing a tightly-fitting, single-breasted blue frock-coat and a pair of pink striped cotton trousers, while the younger candidly displayed the trousers of his brother's suit, as a harmonious change to a shining black alpaca coat and crimson neckerchief. Fairfax, who brought up the rear, had, with characteristic unselfishness, contented himself with a French workman's blue blouse and a pair of white duck trousers. Had they shown the least consciousness of their finery, or of its absurdity, they would have seemed despicable. But only one expression beamed on the five sunburnt and shining faces—a look of unaffected boyish gratification and unrestricted welcome.

They halted before Mr. Carr and his daughters, simultaneously removed their various and remarkable head coverings, and waited until Fairfax advanced and severally presented them. Jessie Carr's half-frightened smile took refuge in the trembling shadows of her dark lashes; Christie Carr stiffened slightly, and looked straight before her.

"We reckoned—that is—we intended to meet you and the young ladies at the grade," said Fairfax, reddening a little as he endeavored to conceal his too ready slang, "and save you from trapesing—from dragging yourselves up grade again to your house."

"Then there IS a house?" said Jessie, with an alarming frank laugh of relief, that was, however, as frankly reflected in the boyishly appreciative eyes of the young men.

"Such as it is," responded Fairfax, with a shade of anxiety, as he glanced at the fresh and pretty costumes of the young women, and dubiously regarded the two Saratoga trunks resting hopelessly on the veranda. "I'm afraid it isn't much, for what you're accustomed to. But," he added more cheerfully, "it will do for a day or two, and perhaps you'll give us the pleasure of showing you the way there now."

The procession was quickly formed. Mr. Carr, alive only to the actual business that had brought him there, at once took possession of Fairfax, and began to disclose his plans for the working of the mine, occasionally halting to look at the work already done in the ditches, and to examine the field of his future operations. Fairfax, not displeased at being thus relieved of a lighter attendance on Mr. Carr's daughters, nevertheless from time to time cast a paternal glance backwards upon their escorts, who had each seized a handle of the two trunks, and were carrying them in couples at the young ladies' side. The occupation did not offer much freedom for easy gallantry, but no sign of discomfiture or uneasiness was visible in the grateful faces of the young men. The necessity of changing hands at times with their burdens brought a corresponding change of cavalier at the lady's side, although it was observed that the younger Kearney, for the sake of continuing a conversation with Miss Jessie, kept his grasp of the handle nearest the young lady until his hand was nearly cut through, and his arm worn out by exhaustion.

"The only thing on wheels in the camp is a mule wagon, and the mules are packin' gravel from the river this afternoon," explained Dick Mattingly apologetically to Christie, "or we'd have toted—I mean carried—you and your baggage up to the shant—the—your house. Give us two weeks more, Miss Carr—only two weeks to wash up our work and realize—and we'll give you a pair of 2.40 steppers and a skeleton buggy to meet you at the top of the hill and drive you over to the cabin. Perhaps you'd prefer a regular carriage; some ladies do. And a nigger driver. But what's the use of planning anything? Afore that time comes we'll have run you up a house on the hill, and you shall pick out the spot. It wouldn't take long—unless you preferred brick. I suppose we could get brick over from La Grange, if you cared for it, but it would take longer. If you could put up for a time with something of stained glass and a mahogany veranda—"

In spite of her cold indignation, and the fact that she could understand only a part of Mattingly's speech, Christie comprehended enough to make her lift her clear eyes to the speaker, as she replied freezingly that she feared she would not trouble them long with her company.

"Oh, you'll get over that," responded Mattingly, with an exasperating confidence that drove her nearly frantic, from the manifest kindliness of intent that made it impossible for her to resent it. "I felt that way myself at first. Things will look strange and unsociable for a while, until you get the hang of them. You'll naturally stamp round and cuss a little—" He stopped in conscious consternation.

With ready tact, and before Christie could reply, Maryland Joe had put down the trunk and changed hands with his brother.

"You mustn't mind Dick, or he'll go off and kill himself with shame," he whispered laughingly in her ear. "He means all right, but he's picked up so much slang here that he's about forgotten how to talk English, and it's nigh on to four years since he's met a young lady."

Christie did not reply. Yet the laughter of her sister in advance with the Kearney brothers seemed to make the reserve with which she tried to crush further familiarity only ridiculous.

"Do you know many operas, Miss Carr?"

She looked at the boyish, interested, sunburnt face so near to her own, and hesitated. After all, why should she add to her other real disappointments by taking this absurd creature seriously?

"In what way?" she returned, with a half smile.

"To play. On the piano, of course. There isn't one nearer here than Sacramento; but I reckon we could get a small one by Thursday. You couldn't do anything on a banjo?" he added doubtfully; "Kearney's got one."

"I imagine it would be very difficult to carry a piano over those mountains," said Christie laughingly, to avoid the collateral of the banjo.

"We got a billiard-table over from Stockton," half bashfully interrupted Dick Mattingly, struggling from his end of the trunk to recover his composure, "and it had to be brought over in sections on the back of a mule, so I don't see why—" He stopped short again in confusion, at a sign from his brother, and then added, "I mean, of course, that a piano is a heap more delicate, and valuable, and all that sort of thing, but it's worth trying for."

"Fairfax was always saying he'd get one for himself, so I reckon it's possible," said Joe.

"Does he play?" asked Christie.

"You bet," said Joe, quite forgetting himself in his enthusiasm. "He can snatch Mozart and Beethoven bald-headed."

In the embarrassing silence that followed this speech the fringe of pine wood nearest the flat was reached. Here there was a rude "clearing," and beneath an enormous pine stood the two recently joined tenements. There was no attempt to conceal the point of junction between Kearney's cabin and the newly-transported saloon from the flat—no architectural illusion of the palpable collusion of the two buildings, which seemed to be telescoped into each other. The front room or living room occupied the whole of Kearney's cabin. It contained, in addition to the necessary articles for house-keeping, a "bunk" or berth for Mr. Carr, so as to leave the second building entirely to the occupation of his daughters as bedroom and boudoir.

There was a half-humorous, half-apologetic exhibition of the rude utensils of the living room, and then the young men turned away as the two girls entered the open door of the second room. Neither Christie nor Jessie could for a moment understand the delicacy which kept these young men from accompanying them into the room they had but a few moments before decorated and arranged with their own hands, and it was not until they turned to thank their strange entertainers that they found that they were gone.

The arrangement of the second room was rude and bizarre, but not without a singular originality and even tastefulness of conception. What had been the counter or "bar" of the saloon, gorgeous in white and gold, now sawn in two and divided, was set up on opposite sides of the room as separate dressing-tables, decorated with huge bunches of azaleas, that hid the rough earthenware bowls, and gave each table the appearance of a vestal altar.

The huge gilt plate-glass mirror which had hung behind the bar still occupied one side of the room, but its length was artfully divided by an enormous rosette of red, white, and blue muslin—one of the surviving Fourth of July decorations of Thompson's saloon. On either side of the door two pathetic-looking, convent-like cots, covered with spotless sheeting, and heaped up in the middle, like a snow-covered grave, had attracted their attention. They were still staring at them when Mr. Carr anticipated their curiosity.

"I ought to tell you that the young men confided to me the fact that there was neither bed nor mattress to be had on the Ford. They have filled some flour sacks with clean dry moss from the woods, and put half a dozen blankets on the top, and they hope you can get along until the messenger who starts to-night for La Grange can bring some bedding over."

Jessie flew with mischievous delight to satisfy herself of the truth of this marvel. "It's so, Christie," she said laughingly—"three flour-sacks apiece; but I'm jealous: yours are all marked 'superfine,' and mine 'middlings.'"

Mr. Carr had remained uneasily watching Christie's shadowed face.

"What matters?" she said drily. "The accommodation is all in keeping."

"It will be better in a day or two," he continued, casting a longing look towards the door—the first refuge of masculine weakness in an impending domestic emergency. "I'll go and see what can be done," he said feebly, with a sidelong impulse towards the opening and freedom. "I've got to see Fairfax again to-night any way."

"One moment, father," said Christie, wearily. "Did you know anything of this place and these—these people—before you came?"

"Certainly—of course I did," he returned, with the sudden testiness of disturbed abstraction. "What are you thinking of? I knew the geological strata and the—the report of Fairfax and his partners before I consented to take charge of the works. And I can tell you that there is a fortune here. I intend to make my own terms, and share in it."

"And not take a salary or some sum of money down?" said Christie, slowly removing her bonnet in the same resigned way.

"I am not a hired man, or a workman, Christie," said her father sharply. "You ought not to oblige me to remind you of that."

"But the hired men—the superintendent and his workmen— were the only ones who ever got anything out of your last experience with Colonel Waters at La Grange, and—and we at least lived among civilized people there."

"These young men are not common people, Christie; even if they have forgotten the restraints of speech and manners, they're gentlemen."

"Who are willing to live like—like negroes."

"You can make them what you please."

Christie raised her eyes. There was a certain cynical ring in her father's voice that was unlike his usual hesitating abstraction. It both puzzled and pained her.

"I mean," he said hastily, "that you have the same opportunity to direct the lives of these young men into more regular, disciplined channels that I have to regulate and correct their foolish waste of industry and material here. It would at least beguile the time for you."

Fortunately for Mr. Carr's escape and Christie's uneasiness, Jessie, who had been examining the details of the living-room, broke in upon this conversation.

"I'm sure it will be as good as a perpetual picnic. George Kearney says we can have a cooking-stove under the tree outside at the back, and as there will be no rain for three months we can do the cooking there, and that will give us more room for—for the piano when it comes; and there's an old squaw to do the cleaning and washing-up any day— and—and—it will be real fun."

She stopped breathlessly, with glowing cheeks and sparkling eyes—a charming picture of youth and trustfulness. Mr. Carr had seized the opportunity to escape.

"Really, now, Christie," said Jessie confidentially, when they were alone, and Christie had begun to unpack her trunk, and to mechanically put her things away, "they're not so bad."

"Who?" asked Christie.

"Why, the Kearneys, and Mattinglys, and Fairfax, and the lot, provided you don't look at their clothes. And think of it! they told me—for they tell one EVERYTHING in the most alarming way—that those clothes were bought to please US. A scramble of things bought at La Grange, without reference to size or style. And to hear these creatures talk, why, you'd think they were Astors or Rothschilds. Think of that little one with the curls—I don't believe he is over seventeen, for all his baby moustache—says he's going to build an assembly hall for us to give a dance in next month; and apologizes the next breath to tell us that there isn't any milk to be had nearer than La Grange, and we must do without it, and use syrup in our tea to-morrow."

"And where is all this wealth?" said Christie, forcing herself to smile at her sister's animation.

"Under our very feet, my child, and all along the river. Why, what we thought was pure and simple mud is what they call 'gold-bearing cement.'"

"I suppose that is why they don't brush their boots and trousers, it's so precious," returned Christie drily. "And have they ever translated this precious dirt into actual coin?"

"Bless you, yes. Why, that dirty little gutter, you know, that ran along the side of the road and followed us down the hill all the way here, that cost them—let me see—yes, nearly sixty thousand dollars. And fancy! papa's just condemned it—says it won't do; and they've got to build another."

An impatient sigh from Christie drew Jessie's attention to her troubled eyebrows.

"Don't worry about our disappointment, dear. It isn't so very great. I dare say we'll be able to get along here in some way, until papa is rich again. You know they intend to make him share with them."

"It strikes me that he is sharing with them already," said Christie, glancing bitterly round the cabin; "sharing every-thing—ourselves, our lives, our tastes."

"Ye-e-s!" said Jessie, with vaguely hesitating assent. "Yes, even these:" she showed two dice in the palm of her little hand. "I found 'em in the drawer of our dressing-table."

"Throw them away," said Christie impatiently.

But Jessie's small fingers closed over the dice. "I'll give them to the little Kearney. I dare say they were the poor boy's playthings."

The appearance of these relics of wild dissipation, however, had lifted Christie out of her sublime resignation. "For Heaven's sake, Jessie," she said, "look around and see if there is anything more!"

To make sure, they each began to scrimmage; the broken-spirited Christie exhibiting both alacrity and penetration in searching obscure corners. In the dining-room, behind the dresser, three or four books were discovered: an odd volume of Thackeray, another of Dickens, a memorandum-book or diary. "This seems to be Latin," said Jessie, fishing out a smaller book. "I can't read it."

"It's just as well you shouldn't," said Christie shortly, whose ideas of a general classical impropriety had been gathered from pages of Lempriere's dictionary. "Put it back directly."

Jessie returned certain odes of one Horatius Flaccus to the corner, and uttered an exclamation. "Oh, Christie! here are some letters tied up with a ribbon."

They were two or three prettily written letters, exhaling a faint odor of refinement and of the pressed flowers that peeped from between the loose leaves. "I see, 'My darling Fairfax.' It's from some woman."

"I don't think much of her, whosoever she is," said Christie, tossing the intact packet back into the corner.

"Nor I," echoed Jessie.

Nevertheless, by some feminine inconsistency, evidently the circumstance did make them think more of HIM, for a minute later, when they had reentered their own room, Christie remarked, "The idea of petting a man by his family name! Think of mamma ever having called papa 'darling Carr'!"

"Oh, but his family name isn't Fairfax," said Jessie hastily; "that's his FIRST name, his Christian name. I forget what's his other name, but nobody ever calls him by it."

"Do you mean," said Christie, with glistening eyes and awful deliberation—"do you mean to say that we're expected to fall in with this insufferable familiarity? I suppose they'll be calling US by our Christian names next."

"Oh, but they do!" said Jessie, mischievously.

"What!"

"They call me Miss Jessie; and Kearney, the little one, asked me if Christie played."

"And what did you say?"

"I said that you did," answered Jessie, with an affectation of cherubic simplicity. "You do, dear; don't you? . . . There, don't get angry, darling; I couldn't flare up all of a sudden in the face of that poor little creature; he looked so absurd—and so—so honest."

Christie turned away, relapsing into her old resigned manner, and assuming her household duties in a quiet, temporizing way that was, however, without hope or expectation.

Mr. Carr, who had dined with his friends under the excuse of not adding to the awkwardness of the first day's house-keeping returned late at night with a mass of papers and drawings, into which he afterwards withdrew, but not until he had delivered himself of a mysterious package entrusted to him by the young men for his daughters. It contained a contribution to their board in the shape of a silver spoon and battered silver mug, which Jessie chose to facetiously consider as an affecting reminiscence of the youthful Kearney's christening days—which it probably was.

The young girls retired early to their white snow-drifts: Jessie not without some hilarious struggles with hers, in which she was, however, quickly surprised by the deep and refreshing sleep of youth; Christie to lie awake and listen to the night wind, that had changed from the first cool whispers of sunset to the sturdy breath of the mountain. At times the frail house shook and trembled. Wandering gusts laden with the deep resinous odors of the wood found their way through the imperfect jointure of the two cabins, swept her cheek and even stirred her long, wide-open lashes. A broken spray of pine needles rustled along the roof, or a pine cone dropped with a quick reverberating tap-tap that for an instant startled her. Lying thus, wide awake, she fell into a dreamy reminiscence of the past, hearing snatches of old melody in the moving pines, fragments of sentences, old words, and familiar epithets in the murmuring wind at her ear, and even the faint breath of long-forgotten kisses on her cheek. She remembered her mother—a pallid creature, who had slowly faded out of one of her father's vague speculations in a vaguer speculation of her own, beyond his ken—whose place she had promised to take at her father's side. The words, "Watch over him, Christie; he needs a woman's care," again echoed in her ears, as if borne on the night wind from the lonely grave in the lonelier cemetery by the distant sea. She had devoted herself to him with some little sacrifices of self, only remembered now for their uselessness in saving her father the disappointment that sprang from his sanguine and one-idea'd temperament. She thought of him lying asleep in the other room, ready on the morrow to devote those fateful qualities to the new enterprise that with equally fateful disposition she believed would end in failure. It did not occur to her that the doubts of her own practical nature were almost as dangerous and illogical as his enthusiasm, and that for that reason she was fast losing what little influence she possessed over him. With the example of her mother's weakness before her eyes, she had become an unsparing and distrustful critic, with the sole effect of awakening his distrust and with-drawing his confidence from her.

He was beginning to deceive her as he had never deceived her mother. Even Jessie knew more of this last enterprise than she did herself.

All that did not tend to decrease her utter restlessness. It was already past midnight when she noticed that the wind had again abated. The mountain breeze had by this time possessed the stifling valleys and heated bars of the river in its strong, cold embraces; the equilibrium of Nature was restored, and a shadowy mist rose from the hollow. A stillness, more oppressive and intolerable than the previous commotion, began to pervade the house and the surrounding woods. She could hear the regular breathing of the sleepers; she even fancied she could detect the faint impulses of the more distant life in the settlement. The far-off barking of a dog, a lost shout, the indistinct murmur of some nearer watercourse—mere phantoms of sound—made the silence more irritating. With a sudden resolution she arose, dressed herself quietly and completely, threw a heavy cloak over her head and shoulders, and opened the door between the living-room and her own. Her father was sleeping soundly in his bunk in the corner. She passed noiselessly through the room, opened the lightly fastened door, and stepped out into the night.

In the irritation and disgust of her walk hither, she had never noticed the situation of the cabin, as it nestled on the slope at the fringe of the woods; in the preoccupation of her disappointment and the mechanical putting away of her things, she had never looked once from the window of her room, or glanced backward out of the door that she had entered. The view before her was a revelation—a reproach, a surprise that took away her breath. Over her shoulders the newly risen moon poured a flood of silvery light, stretching from her feet across the shining bars of the river to the opposite bank, and on up to the very crest of the Devil's Spur—no longer a huge bulk of crushing shadow, but the steady exaltation of plateau, spur, and terrace clothed with replete and unutterable beauty. In this magical light that beauty seemed to be sustained and carried along by the river winding at its base, lifted again to the broad shoulder of the mountain, and lost only in the distant vista of death-like, overcrowning snow. Behind and above where she stood the towering woods seemed to be waiting with opened ranks to absorb her with the little cabin she had quitted, dwarfed into insignificance in the vast prospect; but nowhere was there another sign or indication of human life and habitation. She looked in vain for the settlement, for the rugged ditches, the scattered cabins, and the unsightly heaps of gravel. In the glamour of the moonlight they had vanished; a veil of silver-gray vapor touched here and there with ebony shadows masked its site. A black strip beyond was the river bank. All else was changed. With a sudden sense of awe and loneliness she turned to the cabin and its sleeping inmates—all that seemed left to her in the vast and stupendous domination of rock and wood and sky.

But in another moment the loneliness passed. A new and delicious sense of an infinite hospitality and friendliness in their silent presence began to possess her. This same slighted, forgotten, uncomprehended, but still foolish and forgiving Nature seemed to be bending over her frightened and listening ear with vague but thrilling murmurings of freedom and independence. She felt her heart expand with its wholesome breath, her soul fill with its sustaining truth.

She felt—

What was that?

An unmistakable outburst of a drunken song at the foot of the slope:—

"Oh, my name it is Johnny from Pike,
I'm h-ll on a spree or a strike." . . .

She stopped as crimson with shame and indignation as if the viewless singer had risen before her.

"I knew when to bet, and get up and get—"

"Hush! D—n it all. Don't you hear?"

There was the sound of hurried whispers, a "No" and "Yes," and then a dead silence.

Christie crept nearer to the edge of the slope in the shadow of a buckeye. In the clearer view she could distinguish a staggering figure in the trail below who had evidently been stopped by two other expostulating shadows that were approaching from the shelter of a tree.

"Sho!—didn't know!"

The staggering figure endeavored to straighten itself, and then slouched away in the direction of the settlement. The two mysterious shadows retreated again to the tree, and were lost in its deeper shadow. Christie darted back to the cabin, and softly reentered her room.

"I thought I heard a noise that woke me, and I missed you," said Jessie, rubbing her eyes. "Did you see anything?"

"No," said Christie, beginning to undress.

"You weren't frightened, dear?"

"Not in the least," said Christie, with a strange little laugh. "Go to sleep."

Bret Harte

CHAPTER III

The five impulsive millionaires of Devil's Ford fulfilled not a few of their most extravagant promises. In less than six weeks Mr. Carr and his daughters were installed in a new house, built near the site of the double cabin, which was again transferred to the settlement, in order to give greater seclusion to the fair guests. It was a long, roomy, one-storied villa, with a not unpicturesque combination of deep veranda and trellis work, which relieved the flat monotony of the interior and the barrenness of the freshly-cleared ground. An upright piano, brought from Sacramento, occupied the corner of the parlor. A suite of gorgeous furniture, whose pronounced and extravagant glories the young girls instinctively hid under home-made linen covers, had also been spoils from afar. Elsewhere the house was filled with ornaments and decorations that in their incongruity forcibly recalled the gilded plate-glass mirrors of the bedroom in the old cabin. In the hasty furnishing of this Aladdin's palace, the slaves of the ring had evidently seized upon anything that would add to its glory, without reference always to fitness.

"I wish it didn't look so cussedly like a robber's cave," said George Kearney, when they were taking a quiet preliminary survey of the unclassified treasures, before the Carrs took possession.

"Or a gambling hell," said his brother reflectively.

"It's about the same thing, I reckon," said Dick Mattingly, who was supposed, in his fiery youth, to have encountered the similarity.

Nevertheless, the two girls managed to bestow the heterogeneous collection with tasteful adaptation to their needs. A crystal chandelier, which had once lent a fascinating illusion to the game of Monte, hung unlighted in the broad hall, where a few other bizarre and public articles were relegated. A long red sofa or bench, which had done duty beside a billiard-table found a place here also. Indeed, it is to be feared that some of the more rustic and bashful youths of Devil's Ford, who had felt it incumbent upon them to pay their respects to the new-comers, were more at ease in this vestibule than in the arcana beyond, whose glories they could see through the open door. To others, it represented a recognized state of probation before their re-entree into civilization again. "I reckon, if you don't mind, miss," said the spokesman of one party, "ez this is our first call, we'll sorter hang out in the hall yer, until you'r used to us." On another occasion, one Whiskey Dick, impelled by a sense of duty, paid a visit to the new house and its fair occupants, in a fashion frankly recounted by him afterwards at the bar of the Tecumseh Saloon.

"You see, boys, I dropped in there the other night, when some of you fellers was doin' the high-toned 'thankee, marm' business in the parlor. I just came to anchor in the corner of the sofy in the hall, without lettin' on to say that I was there, and took up a Webster's dictionary that was on the table and laid it open—keerless like, on my knees, ez if I was sorter consultin' it—and kinder dozed off there, listenin' to you fellows gassin' with the young ladies, and that yer Miss Christie just snakin' music outer that pianner, and I reckon I fell asleep. Anyhow, I was there nigh on to two hours. It's mighty soothin', them fashionable calls; sorter knocks the old camp dust outer a fellow, and sets him up again."

It would have been well if the new life of the Devil's Ford had shown no other irregularity than the harmless eccentricities of its original locaters. But the news of its sudden fortune, magnified by report, began presently to flood the settlement with another class of adventurers. A tide of waifs, strays, and malcontents of old camps along the river began to set towards Devil's Ford, in very much the same fashion as the debris, drift, and alluvium had been carried down in bygone days and cast upon its banks. A few immigrant wagons, diverted from the highways of travel by the fame of the new diggings, halted upon the slopes of Devil's Spur and on the arid flats of the Ford, and disgorged their sallow freight of alkali-poisoned, prematurely-aged women and children and maimed and fever-stricken men. Against this rude form of domesticity were opposed the chromo-tinted dresses and extravagant complexions of a few single unattended women—happily seen more often at night behind gilded bars than in the garish light of day—and an equal number of pale-faced, dark-moustached, well-dressed, and suspiciously idle men. A dozen rivals of Thompson's Saloon had sprung up along the narrow main street. There were two new hotels—one a "Temperance House," whose ascetic quality was confined only to the abnegation of whiskey—a rival stage office, and a small one-storied building, from which the "Sierran Banner" fluttered weekly, for "ten dollars a year, in advance." Insufferable in the glare of a Sabbath sun, bleak, windy, and flaring in the gloom of a Sabbath night, and hopelessly depressing on all days of the week, the First Presbyterian Church lifted its blunt steeple from the barrenest area of the flats, and was hideous! The civic improvements so enthusiastically contemplated by the five millionaires in the earlier pages of this veracious chronicle—

the fountain, reservoir, town-hall, and free library—had not yet been erected. Their sites had been anticipated by more urgent buildings and mining works, unfortunately not considered in the sanguine dreams of the enthusiasts, and, more significant still, their cost and expense had been also anticipated by the enormous outlay of their earnings in the work upon Devil's Ditch.

Nevertheless, the liberal fulfilment of their promise in the new house in the suburbs blinded the young girls' eyes to their shortcomings in the town. Their own remoteness and elevation above its feverish life kept them from the knowledge of much that was strange, and perhaps disturbing to their equanimity. As they did not mix with the immigrant women—Miss Jessie's good-natured intrusion into one of their half-nomadic camps one day having been met with rudeness and suspicion—they gradually fell into the way of trusting the responsibility of new acquaintances to the hands of their original hosts, and of consulting them in the matter of local recreation. It thus occurred that one day the two girls, on their way to the main street for an hour's shopping at the Villa de Paris and Variety Store, were stopped by Dick Mattingly a few yards from their house, with the remark that, as the county election was then in progress, it would be advisable for them to defer their intention for a few hours. As he did not deem it necessary to add that two citizens, in the exercise of a freeman's franchise, had been supplementing their ballots with bullets, in front of an admiring crowd, they knew nothing of that accident that removed from Devil's Ford an entertaining stranger, who had only the night before partaken of their hospitality.

A week or two later, returning one morning from a stroll in the forest, Christie and Jessie were waylaid by George Kearney and Fairfax, and, under pretext of being shown a new and romantic trail, were diverted from the regular path.

This enabled Mattingly and Maryland Joe to cut down the body of a man hanged by the Vigilance Committee a few hours before on the regular trail, and to remonstrate with the committee on the incompatibility of such exhibitions with a maidenly worship of nature.

"With the whole county to hang a man in," expostulated Joe, "you might keep clear of Carr's woods."

It is needless to add that the young girls never knew of this act of violence, or the delicacy that kept them in ignorance of it. Mr. Carr was too absorbed in business to give heed to what he looked upon as a convulsion of society as natural as a geological upheaval, and too prudent to provoke the criticism of his daughters by comment in their presence.

An equally unexpected confidence, however, took its place. Mr. Carr having finished his coffee one morning, lingered a moment over his perfunctory paternal embraces, with the awkwardness of a preoccupied man endeavoring by the assumption of a lighter interest to veil another abstraction.

"And what are we doing to-day, Christie?" he asked, as Jessie left the dining-room.

"Oh, pretty much the usual thing—nothing in particular. If George Kearney gets the horses from the summit, we're going to ride over to Indian Spring to picnic. Fairfax—Mr. Munroe—I always forget that man's real name in this dreadfully familiar country—well, he's coming to escort us, and take me, I suppose—that is, if Kearney takes Jessie."

"A very nice arrangement," returned her father, with a slight nervous contraction of the corners of his mouth and eyelids to indicate mischievousness. "I've no doubt they'll both be here. You know they usually are—ha! ha! And what about the two Mattinglys and Philip Kearney, eh?" he continued; "won't they be jealous?"

"It isn't their turn," said Christie carelessly; "besides, they'll probably be there."

"And I suppose they're beginning to be resigned," said Carr, smiling.

"What on earth are you talking of, father?"

She turned her clear brown eyes upon him, and was regarding him with such manifest unconsciousness of the drift of his speech, and, withal, a little vague impatience of his archness, that Mr. Carr was feebly alarmed. It had the effect of banishing his assumed playfulness, which made his serious explanation the more irritating.

"Well, I rather thought that—that young Kearney was paying considerable attention to—to—to Jessie," replied her father, with hesitating gravity.

"What! that boy?"

"Young Kearney is one of the original locators, and an equal partner in the mine. A very enterprising young fellow. In fact, much more advanced and bolder in his conceptions than the others. I find no difficulty with him."

At another time Christie would have questioned the convincing quality of this proof, but she was too much shocked at her father's first suggestion, to think of anything else.

"You don't mean to say, father, that you are talking seriously of these men—your friends—whom we see every day—and our only company?"

"No, no!" said Mr. Carr hastily; "you misunderstand. I don't suppose that Jessie or you—"

"Or ME! Am I included?"

"You don't let me speak, Christie. I mean, I am not talking seriously," continued Mr. Carr, with his most serious aspect, "of you and Jessie in this matter; but it may be a serious thing to these young men to be thrown continually in the company of two attractive girls."

"I understand—you mean that we should not see so much of them," said Christie, with a frank expression of relief so genuine as to utterly discompose her father. "Perhaps you are right, though I fail to discover anything serious in the attentions of young Kearney to Jessie—or—whoever it may be—to me. But it will be very easy to remedy it, and see less of them. Indeed, we might begin to-day with some excuse."

"Yes—certainly. Of course!" said Mr. Carr, fully convinced of his utter failure, but, like most weak creatures, consoling himself with the reflection that he had not shown his hand or committed himself. "Yes; but it would perhaps be just as well for the present to let things go on as they were. We'll talk of it again—I'm in a hurry now," and, edging himself through the door, he slipped away.

"What do you think is father's last idea?" said Christie, with, I fear, a slight lack of reverence in her tone, as her sister reentered the room. "He thinks George Kearney is paying you too much attention."

"No!" said Jessie, replying to her sister's half-interrogative, half-amused glance with a frank, unconscious smile.

"Yes, and he says that Fairfax—I think it's Fairfax—is

equally fascinated with ME."

Jessie's brow slightly contracted as she looked curiously at her sister.

"Of all things," she said, "I wonder if any one has put that idea into his dear old head. He couldn't have thought it himself."

"I don't know," said Christie musingly; "but perhaps it's just as well if we kept a little more to ourselves for a while."

"Did father say so?" said Jessie quickly.

"No, but that is evidently what he meant."

"Ye-es," said Jessie slowly, "unless—"

"Unless what?" said Christie sharply. "Jessie, you don't for a moment mean to say that you could possibly conceive of anything else?"

"I mean to say," said Jessie, stealing her arm around her sister's waist demurely, "that you are perfectly right. We'll keep away from these fascinating Devil's Forders, and particularly the youngest Kearney. I believe there has been some ill-natured gossip. I remember that the other day, when we passed the shanty of that Pike County family on the slope, there were three women at the door, and one of them said something that made poor little Kearney turn white and pink alternately, and dance with suppressed rage. I suppose the old lady—M'Corkle, that's her name—would like to have a share of our cavaliers for her Euphemy and Mamie. I dare say it's only right; I would lend them the cherub occasionally, and you might let them have Mr. Munroe twice a week."

Bret Harte

She laughed, but her eyes sought her sister's with a certain watchfulness of expression.

Christie shrugged her shoulders, with a suggestion of disgust.

"Don't joke. We ought to have thought of all this before."

"But when we first knew them, in the dear old cabin, there wasn't any other woman and nobody to gossip, and that's what made it so nice. I don't think so very much of civilization, do you?" said the young lady pertly.

Christie did not reply. Perhaps she was thinking the same thing. It certainly had been very pleasant to enjoy the spontaneous and chivalrous homage of these men, with no further suggestion of recompense or responsibility than the permission to be worshipped; but beyond that she racked her brain in vain to recall any look or act that proclaimed the lover. These men, whom she had found so relapsed into barbarism that they had forgotten the most ordinary forms of civilization; these men, even in whose extravagant admiration there was a certain loss of self-respect, that as a woman she would never forgive; these men, who seemed to belong to another race—impossible! Yet it was so.

"What construction must they have put upon her father's acceptance of their presents—of their company—of her free-dom in their presence? No! they must have understood from the beginning that she and her sister had never looked upon them except as transient hosts and chance acquaintances. Any other idea was preposterous. And yet—"

It was the recurrence of this "yet" that alarmed her. For she remembered now that but for their slavish devotion they might claim to be her equal. According to her father's account, they had come from homes as good as their own; they were certainly more than her equal in fortune; and her father had come to them as an employee, until they had taken him into partnership. If there had only been sentiment of any kind connected with any of them! But they were all alike, brave, unselfish, humorous—and often ridiculous. If anything, Dick Mattingly was funniest by nature, and made her laugh more. Maryland Joe, his brother, told better stories (sometimes of Dick), though not so good a mimic as the other Kearney, who had a fairly sympathetic voice in singing. They were all good-looking enough; perhaps they set store on that—men are so vain.

And as for her own rejected suitor, Fairfax Munroe, except for a kind of grave and proper motherliness about his protecting manner, he absolutely was the most indistinctive of them all. He had once brought her some rare tea from the Chinese camp, and had taught her how to make it; he had cautioned her against sitting under the trees at nightfall; he had once taken off his coat to wrap around her. Really, if this were the only evidence of devotion that could be shown, she was safe!

"Well," said Jessie, "it amuses you, I see."

Christie checked the smile that had been dimpling the cheek nearest Jessie, and turned upon her the face of an elder sister.

"Tell me, have YOU noticed this extraordinary attention of Mr. Munroe to me?"

"Candidly?" asked Jessie, seating herself comfortably on the table sideways, and endeavoring, to pull her skirt over her little feet. "Honest Injun?"

"Don't be idiotic, and, above all, don't be slangy! Of course, candidly."

"Well, no. I can't say that I have."

"Then," said Christie, "why in the name of all that's preposterous, do they persist in pairing me off with the least interesting man of the lot?"

Jessie leaped from the table.

"Come now," she said, with a little nervous laugh, "he's not so bad as all that. You don't know him. But what does it matter now, as long as we're not going to see them any more?"

"They're coming here for the ride to-day," said Christie resignedly. "Father thought it better not to break it off at once."

"Father thought so!" echoed Jessie, stopping with her hand on the door.

"Yes; why do you ask?"

But Jessie had already left the room, and was singing in the hall.

CHAPTER IV

The afternoon did not, however, bring their expected visitors. It brought, instead, a brief note by the hands of Whiskey Dick from Fairfax, apologizing for some business that kept him and George Kearney from accompanying the ladies. It added that the horses were at the disposal of themselves and any escort they might select, if they would kindly give the message to Whiskey Dick.

The two girls looked at each other awkwardly; Jessie did not attempt to conceal a slight pout.

"It looks as if they were anticipating us," she said, with a half-forced smile. "I wonder, now, if there really has been any gossip? But no! They wouldn't have stopped for that, unless—" She looked curiously at her sister.

"Unless what?" repeated Christie; "you are horribly mysterious this morning."

"Am I? It's nothing. But they're wanting an answer. Of course you'll decline."

"And intimate we only care for their company! No! We'll say we're sorry they can't come, and—accept their horses. We can do without an escort, we two."

"Capital!" said Jessie, clapping her hands. "We'll show them—"

"We'll show them nothing," interrupted Christie decidedly. "In our place there's only the one thing to do. Where is this—Whiskey Dick?"

"In the parlor."

"The parlor!" echoed Christie. "Whiskey Dick? What—is he—"

"Yes; he's all right," said Jessie confidently. "He's been here before, but he stayed in the hall; he was so shy. I don't think you saw him."

"I should think not—Whiskey Dick!"

"Oh, you can call him Mr. Hall, if you like," said Jessie, laughing. "His real name is Dick Hall. If you want to be funny, you can say Alky Hall, as the others do."

Christie's only reply to this levity was a look of superior resignation as she crossed the hall and entered the parlor.

Then ensued one of those surprising, mystifying, and utterly inexplicable changes that leave the masculine being so helpless in the hands of his feminine master. Before Christie opened the door her face underwent a rapid transformation: the gentle glow of a refined woman's welcome suddenly beamed in her interested eyes; the impulsive courtesy of an expectant hostess eagerly seizing a long-looked-for opportunity broke in a smile upon her lips as she swept across the room, and stopped with her two white outstretched hands before Whiskey Dick.

It needed only the extravagant contrast presented by that gentleman to complete the tableau. Attired in a suit of shining black alpaca, the visitor had evidently prepared himself with some care for a possible interview. He was seated by the French window opening upon the veranda, as if to secure a retreat in case of an emergency. Scrupulously washed and shaven, some of the soap appeared to have lingered in his eyes and inflamed the lids, even while it lent a sleek and shining lustre, not unlike his coat, to his smooth black hair. Nevertheless, leaning back in his chair, he had allowed a large white handkerchief to depend gracefully from his fingers—a pose at once suggesting easy and elegant langour.

"How kind of you to give me an opportunity to make up for my misfortune when you last called! I was so sorry to have missed you. But it was entirely my fault! You were hurried, I think—you conversed with others in the hall—you—"

She stopped to assist him to pick up the handkerchief that had fallen, and the Panama hat that had rolled from his lap towards the window when he had started suddenly to his feet at the apparition of grace and beauty. As he still nervously retained the two hands he had grasped, this would have been a difficult feat, even had he not endeavored at the same moment, by a backward furtive kick, to propel the hat out of the window, at which she laughingly broke from his grasp and flew to the rescue.

"Don't mind it, miss," he said hurriedly. "It is not worth your demeaning yourself to touch it. Leave it outside thar, miss. I wouldn't have toted it in, anyhow, if some of those high-falutin' fellows hadn't allowed, the other night, ez it were the reg'lar thing to do; as if, miss, any gentleman kalkilated to ever put on his hat in the house afore a lady!"

But Christie had already possessed herself of the unlucky object, and had placed it upon the table. This compelled Whiskey Dick to rise again, and as an act of careless good breeding to drop his handkerchief in it. He then leaned one elbow upon the piano, and, crossing one foot over the other, remained standing in an attitude he remembered to have seen in the pages of an illustrated paper as portraying the hero in some drawing-room scene. It was easy and effective, but seemed to be more favorable to revery than conversation. Indeed, he remembered that he had forgotten to consult the letterpress as to which it represented.

"I see you agree with me, that politeness is quite a matter of intention," said Christie, "and not of mere fashion and rules. Now, for instance," she continued, with a dazzling smile, "I suppose, according to the rules, I ought to give you a note to Mr. Munroe, accepting his offer. That is all that is required; but it seems so much nicer, don't you think, to tell it to YOU for HIM, and have the pleasure of your company and a little chat at the same time."

"That's it, that's just it, Miss Carr; you've hit it in the centre this time," said Whiskey Dick, now quite convinced that his attitude was not intended for eloquence, and shifting back to his own seat, hat and all; "that's tantamount to what I said to the boys just now. 'You want an excuse,' sez I, 'for not goin' out with the young ladies. So, accorden' to rules, you writes a letter allowin' buzziness and that sorter thing detains you. But wot's the facts? You're a gentleman, and as gentlemen you and George comes to the opinion that you're rather playin' it for all it's worth in this yer house, you know— comin' here night and day, off and on, reg'lar sociable and fam'ly like, and makin' people talk about things they ain't any call to talk about, and, what's a darned sight more, YOU FELLOWS ain't got any right YET to allow 'em to talk about, d'ye see?" he paused, out of breath.

It was Miss Christie's turn to move about. In changing her seat to the piano-stool, so as to be nearer her visitor, she brushed down some loose music, which Whiskey Dick hastened to pick up.

"Pray don't mind it," she said, "pray don't, really—let it be— "But Whiskey Dick, feeling himself on safe ground in this attention, persisted to the bitter end of a disintegrated and well-worn "Travatore." "So that is what Mr. Munroe said," she remarked quietly.

"Not just then, in course, but it's what's bin on his mind and in his talk for days off and on," returned Dick, with a knowing smile and a nod of mysterious confidence. "Bless your soul, Miss Carr, folks like you and me don't need to have them things explained. That's what I said to him, sez I. 'Don't send no note, but just go up there and hev it out fair and square, and say what you do mean.' But they would hev the note, and I kalkilated to bring it. But when I set my eyes on you, and heard you express yourself as you did just now, I sez to myself, sez I, 'Dick, yer's a young lady, and a fash'nable lady at that, ez don't go foolin' round on rules and etiketts'—excuse my freedom, Miss Carr—'and you and her, sez I, 'kin just discuss this yer matter in a sociable, off-hand, fash'nable way.' They're a good lot o' boys, Miss Carr, a square lot—white men all of 'em; but they're a little soft and green, may be, from livin' in these yer pine woods along o' the other sap. They just worship the ground you and your sister tread on—certain! of course! of course!" he added hurriedly, recognizing Christie's half-conscious, deprecating gesture with more exaggerated deprecation. "I understand. But what I wanter say is that they'd be willin' to be that ground, and lie down and let you walk over them—so to speak, Miss Carr, so to speak—if it would keep the hem of your gown from gettin' soiled in the mud o' the camp. But it wouldn't do for them to make a reg'lar curderoy road o' themselves for the houl camp to trapse over, on the mere chance of your some time passin' that way, would it now?"

"Won't you let me offer you some refreshment, Mr. Hall?" said Christie, rising, with a slight color. "I'm really ashamed of my forgetfulness again, but I'm afraid it's partly YOUR fault for entertaining me to the exclusion of yourself. No, thank you, let me fetch it for you."

She turned to a handsome sideboard near the door, and presently faced him again with a decanter of whiskey and a glass in her hand, and a return of the bewitching smile she had worn on entering.

"But perhaps you don't take whiskey?" suggested the arch deceiver, with a sudden affected but pretty perplexity of eye, brow, and lips.

For the first time in his life Whiskey Dick hesitated between two forms of intoxication. But he was still nervous and uneasy; habit triumphed, and he took the whiskey. He, however, wiped his lips with a slight wave of his handkerchief, to support a certain easy elegance which he firmly believed relieved the act of any vulgar quality.

"Yes, ma'am," he continued, after an exhilarated pause. "Ez I said afore, this yer's a matter you and me can discuss after the fashion o' society. My idea is that these yer boys should kinder let up on you and Miss Jessie for a while, and do a little more permiskus attention round the Ford. There's one or two families yer with grown-up gals ez oughter be squared; that is—the boys mighter put in a few fancy touches among them—kinder take 'em buggy riding—or to church— once in a while—just to take the pizen outer their tongues, and make a kind o' bluff to the parents, d'ye see? That would sorter divert their own minds; and even if it didn't, it would kinder get 'em accustomed agin to the old style and their own kind. I want to warn ye agin an idea that might occur to you in a giniral way. I don't say you hev the idea, but it's kind o' nat'ral you might be thinkin' of it some time, and I thought I'd warn you agin it."

"I think we understand each other too well to differ much, Mr. Hall," said Christie, still smiling; "but what is the idea?"

The delicate compliment to their confidential relations and the slight stimulus of liquor had tremulously exalted Whiskey Dick. Affecting to look cautiously out of the window and around the room, he ventured to draw nearer the young woman with a half-paternal, half-timid familiarity.

"It might have occurred to you," he said, laying his handkerchief as if to veil mere vulgar contact, on Christie's shoulder, "that it would be a good thing on YOUR side to invite down some of your high-toned gentlemen friends from 'Frisco to visit you and escort you round. It seems quite nat'ral like, and I don't say it ain't, but—the boys wouldn't stand for it."

In spite of her self-possession, Christie's eyes suddenly darkened, and she involuntarily drew herself up. But Whiskey Dick, guiltily attributing the movement to his own indiscreet gesture, said, "Excuse me, miss," recovered himself by lightly dusting her shoulder with his handkerchief, as if to remove the impression, and her smile returned.

"They wouldn't stand for it," said Dick, "and there'd be some shooting! Not afore you, miss—not afore you, in course! But they'd adjourn to the woods some morning with them city folks, and hev it out with rifles at a hundred yards. Or, seein' ez they're city folks, the boys would do the square thing with pistols at twelve paces. They're good boys, as I said afore; but they're quick and tetchy—George, being the youngest, nat'rally is the tetchiest. You know how it is, Miss Carr; his pretty, gal-like face and little moustaches haz cost him half a dozen scrimmages already. He'z had a fight for every hair that's growed in his moustache since he kem here."

"Say no more, Mr. Hall!" said Christie, rising and pressing her hands lightly on Dick's tremulous fingers. "If I ever had any such idea, I should abandon it now; you are quite right in this as in your other opinions. I shall never cease to be thankful to Mr. Munroe and Mr. Kearney that they intrusted this delicate matter to your hands."

"Well," said the gratified and reddening visitor, "it ain't perhaps the square thing to them or myself to say that they reckoned to have me discuss their delicate affairs for them, but—"

"I understand," interrupted Christie. "They simply gave you the letter as a friend. It was my good fortune to find you a sympathizing and liberal man of the world." The delighted Dick, with conscious vanity beaming from every feature of his shining face, lightly waved the compliment aside with his handkerchief, as she continued, "But I am forgetting the message. We accept the horses. Of course we COULD do without an escort; but forgive my speaking so frankly, are YOU engaged this afternoon?"

"Excuse me, miss, I don't take—" stammered Dick, scarcely believing his ears.

"Could you give us your company as an escort?" repeated Christie with a smile.

Was he awake or dreaming, or was this some trick of liquor in his often distorted fancy? He, Whiskey Dick! the butt of his friends, the chartered oracle of the barrooms, even in whose wretched vanity there was always the haunting suspicion that he was despised and scorned; he, who had dared so much in speech, and achieved so little in fact! he, whose habitual weakness had even led him into the wildest indiscretion here; he—now offered a reward for that indiscretion! He, Whiskey Dick, the solicited escort of these two beautiful and peerless girls! What would they say at the Ford? What would his friends think? It would be all over the Ford the next day. His past would be vindicated, his future secured. He grew erect at the thought. It was almost in other voice, and with no trace of his previous exaggeration, that he said, "With pleasure."

"Then, if you will bring the horses at once, we shall be ready when you return."

In another instant he had vanished, as if afraid to trust the reality of his good fortune to the dangers of delay. At the end of half an hour he reappeared, leading the two horses, himself mounted on a half-broken mustang. A pair of large, jingling silver spurs and a stiff sombrero, borrowed with the mustang from some mysterious source, were donned to do honor to the occasion.

The young girls were not yet ready, but he was shown by the Chinese servant into the parlor to wait for them. The decanter of whiskey and glasses were still invitingly there. He was hot, trembling, and flushed with triumph. He walked to the table and laid his hand on the decanter, when an odd thought flashed upon him. He would not drink this time. No, it should not be said that he, the selected escort of the elite of Devil's Ford, had to fill himself up with whiskey before they started. The boys might turn to each other in their astonishment, as he proudly passed with his fair companions, and say, "It's Whiskey Dick," but he'd be d—d if they should add, "and full as ever." No, sir! Nor when he was riding

Bret Harte

beside these real ladies, and leaning over them at some confidential moment, should they even know it from his breath! No. . . . Yet a thimbleful, taken straight, only a thimbleful, wouldn't be much, and might help to pull him together. He again reached his trembling hand for the decanter, hesitated, and then, turning his back upon it, resolutely walked to the open window. Almost at the same instant he found himself face to face with Christie on the veranda.

She looked into his bloodshot eyes, and cast a swift glance at the decanter.

"Won't you take something before you go?" she said sweetly.

"I—reckon—not, jest now," stammered Whiskey Dick, with a heroic effort.

"You're right," said Christie. "I see you are like me. It's too hot for anything fiery. Come with me."

She led him into the dining-room, and pouring out a glass of iced tea handed it to him. Poor Dick was not prepared for this terrible culmination. Whiskey Dick and iced tea! But under pretence of seeing if it was properly flavored, Christie raised it to her own lips.

"Try it, to please me."

He drained the goblet.

"Now, then," said Christie gayly, "let's find Jessie, and be off!"

CHAPTER V

Whatever might have been his other deficiencies as an escort, Whiskey Dick was a good horseman, and, in spite of his fractious brute, exhibited such skill and confidence as to at once satisfy the young girls of his value to them in the management of their own horses, to whom side-saddles were still an alarming novelty. Jessie, who had probably already learned from her sister the purport of Dick's confidences, had received him with equal cordiality and perhaps a more unqualified amusement; and now, when fairly lifted into the saddle by his tremulous but respectful hands, made a very charming picture of youthful and rosy satisfaction. And when Christie, more fascinating than ever in her riding-habit, took her place on the other side of Dick, as they sallied from the gate, that gentleman felt his cup of happiness complete. His triumphal entree into the world of civilization and fashion was secure. He did not regret the untasted liquor; here was an experience in after years to lean his back against comfortably in bar-rooms, to entrance or defy mankind. He had even got so far as to formulate in fancy the sentence: "I remember, gentlemen, that one afternoon, being on a pasear with two fash'nable young ladies," etc., etc.

At present, however, he was obliged to confine himself to the functions of an elegant guide and cicerone—when not engaged in "having it out" with his horse. Their way lay

Bret Harte

along the slope, crossing the high-road at right angles, to reach the deeper woods beyond. Dick would have lingered on the highway—ostensibly to point out to his companions the new flume that had taken the place of the condemned ditch, but really in the hope of exposing himself in his glory to the curious eyes of the wayfaring world.

Unhappily the road was deserted in the still powerful sunlight, and he was obliged to seek the cover of the woods, with a passing compliment to the parent of his charges. Waving his hands towards the flume, he said, "Look at that work of your father's; there ain't no other man in Californy but Philip Carr ez would hev the grit to hold up such a bluff agin natur and agin luck ez that yer flume stands for. I don't say it 'cause you're his daughters, ladies! That ain't the style, ez YOU know, in sassiety, Miss Carr," he added, turning to Christie as the more socially experienced. "No! but there ain't another man to be found ez could do it. It cost already two hundred thousand; it'll cost five hundred thousand afore it's done; and every cent of it is got out of the yearth beneath it, or HEZ got to be out of it. 'Tain't ev'ry man, Miss Carr, ez hev got the pluck to pledge not only what he's got, but what he reckons to git."

"But suppose he don't get it?" said Christie, slightly contracting her brows.

"Then there's the flume to show for it," said Dick.

"But of what use is the flume, if there isn't any more gold?" continued Christie, almost angrily.

"That's good from YOU, miss," said Dick, giving way to a fit of hilarity. "That's good for a fash'nable young lady—own daughter of Philip Carr. She sez, says she," continued Dick, appealing to the sedate pines for appreciation of Christie's rare humor, "'Wot's the use of a flume, when gold ain't there?' I must tell that to the boys."

"And what's the use of the gold in the ground when the flume isn't there to work it out?" said Jessie to her sister, with a cautioning glance towards Dick.

But Dick did not notice the look that passed between the sisters. The richer humor of Jessie's retort had thrown him into convulsions of laughter.

"And now SHE says, wot's the use o' the gold without the flume? 'Xcuse me, ladies, but that's just puttin' the hull question that's agitatin' this yer camp inter two speeches as clear as crystal. There's the hull crowd outside—and some on 'em inside, like Fairfax, hez their doubts—ez says with Miss Christie; and there's all of us inside, ez holds Miss Jessie's views."

"I never heard Mr. Munroe say that the flume was wrong," said Jessie quickly.

"Not to you, nat'rally," said Dick, with a confidential look at Christie; "but I reckon he'd like some of the money it cost laid out for suthin' else. But what's the odds? The gold is there, and WE'RE bound to get it."

Dick was the foreman of a gang of paid workmen, who had replaced the millionaires in mere manual labor, and the WE was a polite figure of speech.

The conversation seemed to have taken an unfortunate turn, and both the girls experienced a feeling of relief when they entered the long gulch or defile that led to Indian Spring. The track now becoming narrow, they were obliged to pass in single file along the precipitous hillside, led by this escort.

This effectually precluded any further speech, and Christie at once surrendered herself to the calm, obliterating influences of the forest. The settlement and its gossip were far behind and forgotten. In the absorption of nature, her companions passed out of her mind, even as they sometimes passed out of her sight in the windings of the shadowy trail. As she rode alone, the fronds of breast-high ferns seemed to caress her with outstretched and gently-detaining hands; strange wildflowers sprang up through the parting underbrush; even the granite rocks that at times pressed closely upon the trail appeared as if cushioned to her contact with star-rayed mosses, or lightly flung after her long lassoes of delicate vines. She recalled the absolute freedom of their al-fresco life in the old double cabin, when she spent the greater part of her waking hours under the mute trees in the encompassing solitude, and, half regretting the more civilized restraints of this newer and more ambitious abode, forgot that she had ever rebelled against it. The social complication that threatened her now seemed to her rather the outcome of her half-civilized parlor than of the sylvan glade. How easy it would have been to have kept the cabin, and then to have gone away entirely, than for her father to have allowed them to be compromised with the growing fortunes of the settlement! The suspicions and distrust that she had always felt of their fortunes seemed to grow with the involuntary admission of Whiskey Dick that they were shared by others who were practical men. She was fain to have recourse to the prospect again to banish these thoughts, and this opened her eyes to the fact that her companions had been missing from the trail ahead of her for some time. She quickened her pace slightly to reach a projecting point of rock that gave her a more extended prospect. But they had evidently disappeared.

She was neither alarmed nor annoyed. She could easily overtake them soon, for they would miss her, and return or wait for her at the spring. At the worst she would have no difficulty in retracing her steps home. In her present mood, she could readily spare their company; indeed she was not sorry that no other being should interrupt that sympathy with the free woods which was beginning to possess her.

She was destined, however, to be disappointed. She had not proceeded a hundred yards before she noticed the moving figure of a man beyond her in the hillside chaparral above the trail. He seemed to be going in the same direction as herself, and, as she fancied, endeavoring to avoid her. This excited her curiosity to the point of urging her horse forward until the trail broadened into the level forest again, which she now remembered was a part of the environs of Indian Spring. The stranger hesitated, pausing once or twice with his back towards her, as if engaged in carefully examining the dwarf willows to select a switch. Christie slightly checked her speed as she drew nearer; when, as if obedient to a sudden resolution, he turned and advanced towards her. She was relieved and yet surprised to recognize the boyish face and figure of George Kearney. He was quite pale and agitated, although attempting, by a jaunty swinging of the switch he had just cut, to assume the appearance of ease and confidence.

Here was an opportunity. Christie resolved to profit by it. She did not doubt that the young fellow had already passed her sister on the trail, but, from bashfulness, had not dared to approach her. By inviting his confidence, she would doubtless draw something from him that would deny or corroborate her father's opinion of his sentiments. If he was really in love with Jessie, she would learn what reasons he had for expecting a serious culmination of his suit, and perhaps she might be able delicately to open his eyes to the truth. If, as she believed, it was only a boyish fancy, she would laugh him out of it with that camaraderie which had always existed between them. A half motherly sympathy, albeit born quite as much from a contemplation of his beautiful yearning eyes as from his interesting position, lightened the smile with which she greeted him.

"So you contrived to throw over your stupid business and join us, after all," she said; "or was it that you changed your mind at the last moment?" she added mischievously. "I thought only we women were permitted that!" Indeed, she could not help noticing that there was really a strong feminine suggestion in the shifting color and slightly conscious eyelids of the young fellow.

"Do young girls always change their minds?" asked George, with an embarrassed smile.

"Not, always; but sometimes they don't know their own mind—particularly if they are very young; and when they do at last, you clever creatures of men, who have interpreted their ignorance to please yourselves, abuse them for being fickle." She stopped to observe the effect of what she believed a rather clear and significant exposition of Jessie's and George's possible situation. But she was not prepared for the look of blank resignation that seemed to drive the color from his face and moisten the fire of his dark eyes.

"I reckon you're right," he said, looking down.

"Oh! we're not accusing you of fickleness," said Christie gayly; "although you didn't come, and we were obliged to ask Mr. Hall to join us. I suppose you found him and Jessie just now?"

But George made no reply. The color was slowly coming back to his face, which, as she glanced covertly at him, seemed to have grown so much older that his returning blood might have brought two or three years with it.

"Really, Mr. Kearney," she said dryly, "one would think that some silly, conceited girl"—she was quite earnest in her epithets, for a sudden, angry conviction of some coquetry and disingenuousness in Jessie had come to her in contemplating its effects upon the young fellow at her side— "some country jilt, had been trying her rustic hand upon you."

"She is not silly, conceited, nor countrified," said George, slowly raising his beautiful eyes to the young girl half reproachfully. "It is I who am all that. No, she is right, and you know it."

Much as Christie admired and valued her sister's charms, she thought this was really going too far. What had Jessie ever done—what was Jessie—to provoke and remain insensible to such a blind devotion as this? And really, looking at him now, he was not so VERY YOUNG for Jessie; whether his unfortunate passion had brought out all his latent manliness, or whether he had hitherto kept his serious nature in the background, certainly he was not a boy. And certainly his was not a passion that he could be laughed out of. It was getting very tiresome. She wished she had not met him—at least until she had had some clearer understanding with her sister. He was still walking beside her, with his hand on her bridle rein, partly to lead her horse over some boulders in the trail, and partly to conceal his first embarrassment. When they had fairly reached the woods, he stopped.

"I am going to say good-by, Miss Carr."

"Are you not coming further? We must be near Indian Spring, now; Mr. Hall and—and Jessie—cannot be far away. You will keep me company until we meet them?"

"No," he replied quietly. "I only stopped you to say good-by.

I am going away."

"Not from Devil's Ford?" she asked, in half-incredulous astonishment. "At least, not for long?"

"I am not coming back," he replied.

"But this is very abrupt," she said hurriedly, feeling that in some ridiculous way she had precipitated an equally ridiculous catastrophe. "Surely you are not going away in this fashion, without saying good-by to Jessie and—and father?"

"I shall see your father, of course—and you will give my regards to Miss Jessie."

He evidently was in earnest. Was there ever anything so perfectly preposterous? She became indignant.

"Of course," she said coldly, "I won't detain you; your business must be urgent, and I forgot—at least I had forgotten until to-day—that you have other duties more important than that of squire of dames. I am afraid this forgetfulness made me think you would not part from us in quite such a business fashion. I presume, if you had not met me just now, we should none of us have seen you again?"

He did not reply.

"Will you say good-by, Miss Carr?"

He held out his hand.

"One moment, Mr. Kearney. If I have said anything which you think justifies this very abrupt leave-taking, I beg you will forgive and forget it—or, at least, let it have no more weight with you than the idle words of any woman. I only spoke generally. You know—I—I might be mistaken."

His eyes, which had dilated when she began to speak, darkened; his color, which had quickly come, as quickly sank when she had ended.

"Don't say that, Miss Carr. It is not like you, and—it is useless. You know what I meant a moment ago. I read it in your reply. You meant that I, like others, had deceived myself. Did you not?"

She could not meet those honest eyes with less than equal honesty. She knew that Jessie did not love him—would not marry him—whatever coquetry she might have shown.

"I did not mean to offend you," she said hesitatingly; "I only half suspected it when I spoke."

"And you wish to spare me the avowal?" he said bitterly.

"To me, perhaps, yes, by anticipating it. I could not tell what ideas you might have gathered from some indiscreet frankness of Jessie—or my father," she added, with almost equal bitterness.

"I have never spoken to either," he replied quickly. He stopped, and added, after a moment's mortifying reflection, "I've been brought up in the woods, Miss Carr, and I suppose I have followed my feelings, instead of the etiquette of society."

Christie was too relieved at the rehabilitation of Jessie's truthfulness to notice the full significance of his speech.

"Good-by," he said again, holding out his hand.

"Good-by!"

She extended her own, ungloved, with a frank smile. He held it for a moment, with his eyes fixed upon hers. Then suddenly, as if obeying an uncontrollable impulse, he crushed it like a flower again and again against his burning lips, and darted away.

Christie sank back in her saddle with a little cry, half of pain and half of frightened surprise. Had the poor boy suddenly gone mad, or was this vicarious farewell a part of the courtship of Devil's Ford? She looked at her little hand, which had reddened under the pressure, and suddenly felt the flush extending to her cheeks and the roots of her hair. This was intolerable.

"Christie!"

It was her sister emerging from the wood to seek her. In another moment she was at her side.

"We thought you were following," said Jessie. "Good heavens! how you look! What has happened?"

"Nothing. I met Mr. Kearney a moment ago on the trail. He is going away, and—and—" She stopped, furious and flushing.

"And," said Jessie, with a burst of merriment, "he told you at last he loved you. Oh, Christie!"

CHAPTER VI

The abrupt departure of George Kearney from Devil's Ford excited but little interest in the community, and was soon forgotten. It was generally attributed to differences between himself and his partners on the question of further outlay of their earnings on mining improvements—he and Philip Carr alone representing a sanguine minority whose faith in the future of the mine accepted any risks. It was alleged by some that he had sold out to his brother; it was believed by others that he had simply gone to Sacramento to borrow money on his share, in order to continue the improvements on his own responsibility. The partners themselves were uncommunicative; even Whiskey Dick, who since his remarkable social elevation had become less oracular, much to his own astonishment, contributed nothing to the gossip except a suggestion that as the fiery temper of George Kearney brooked no opposition, even from his brother, it was better they should separate before the estrangement became serious.

Mr. Carr did not disguise his annoyance at the loss of his young disciple and firm ally. But an unlucky allusion to his previous remarks on Kearney's attentions to Jessie, and a querulous regret that he had permitted a disruption of their social intimacy, brought such an ominous and frigid opposition, not only from Christie, but even the frivolous

Jessie herself, that Carr sank back in a crushed and terrified silence. "I only meant to say," he stammered after a pause, in which he, however, resumed his aggrieved manner, "that FAIRFAX seems to come here still, and HE is not such a particular friend of mine."

"But she is—and has your interest entirely at heart," said Jessie, stoutly, "and he only comes here to tell us how things are going on at the works."

"And criticise your father, I suppose," said Mr. Carr, with an attempt at jocularity that did not, however, disguise an irritated suspiciousness. "He really seems to have supplanted ME as he has poor Kearney in your estimation."

"Now, father," said Jessie, suddenly seizing him by the shoulders in affected indignation, but really to conceal a certain embarrassment that sprang quite as much from her sister's quietly observant eye as her father's speech, "you promised to let this ridiculous discussion drop. You will make me and Christie so nervous that we will not dare to open the door to a visitor, until he declares his innocence of any matrimonial intentions. You don't want to give color to the gossip that agreement with your views about the improvements is necessary to getting on with us."

"Who dares talk such rubbish?" said Carr, reddening; "is that the kind of gossip that Fairfax brings here?"

"Hardly, when it's known that he don't quite agree with you, and DOES come here. That's the best denial of the gossip."

Christie, who had of late loftily ignored these discussions, waited until her father had taken his departure.

"Then that is the reason why you still see Mr. Munroe, after what you said," she remarked quietly to Jessie.

Jessie, who would have liked to escape with her father, was obliged to pause on the threshold of the door, with a pretty assumption of blank forgetfulness in her blue eyes and lifted eyebrows.

"Said what? when?" she asked vacantly.

"When—when Mr. Kearney that day—in the woods—went away," said Christie, faintly coloring.

"Oh! THAT day," said Jessie briskly; "the day he just gloved your hand with kisses, and then fled wildly into the forest to conceal his emotion."

"The day he behaved very foolishly," said Christie, with reproachful calmness, that did not, however, prevent a suspicion of indignant moisture in her eyes—"when you explained"—

"That it wasn't meant for ME," interrupted Jessie.

"That it was to you that MR. MUNROE'S attentions were directed. And then we agreed that it was better to prevent any further advances of this kind by avoiding any familiar relations with either of them."

"Yes," said Jessie, "I remember; but you're not confounding my seeing Fairfax occasionally now with that sort of thing. HE doesn't kiss my hand like anything," she added, as if in abstract reflection.

"Nor run away, either," suggested the trodden worm, turning.

There was an ominous silence.

Bret Harte

"Do you know we are nearly out of coffee?" said Jessie choking, but moving towards the door with Spartan-like calmness.

"Yes. And something must be done this very day about the washing," said Christie, with suppressed emotion, going towards the opposite entrance.

Tears stood in each other's eyes with this terrible exchange of domestic confidences. Nevertheless, after a moment's pause, they deliberately turned again, and, facing each other with frightful calmness, left the room by purposeless and deliberate exits other than those they had contemplated—a crushing abnegation of self, that, to some extent, relieved their surcharged feelings.

Meantime the material prosperity of Devil's Ford increased, if a prosperity based upon no visible foundation but the confidences and hopes of its inhabitants could be called material. Few, if any, stopped to consider that the improvements, buildings, and business were simply the outlay of capital brought from elsewhere, and as yet the settlement or town, as it was now called, had neither produced nor exported capital of itself equal to half the amount expended. It was true that some land was cultivated on the further slope, some mills erected and lumber furnished from the inexhaustible forest; but the consumers were the inhabitants themselves, who paid for their produce in borrowed capital or unlimited credit. It was never discovered that while all roads led to Devil's Ford, Devil's Ford led to nowhere. The difficulties overcome in getting things into the settlement were never surmounted for getting things out of it. The lumber was practically valueless for export to other settlements across the mountain roads, which were equally rich in timber. The theory so enthusiastically held by the original locators, that Devil's Ford was a vast sink that had, through ages, exhausted and absorbed the trickling wealth of the adjacent hills and valleys, was suffering an ironical corroboration.

One morning it was known that work was stopped at the Devil's Ford Ditch—temporarily only, it was alleged, and many of the old workmen simply had their labor for the present transferred to excavating the river banks, and the collection of vast heaps of "pay gravel." Specimens from these mounds, taken from different localities, and at different levels, were sent to San Francisco for more rigid assay and analysis. It was believed that this would establish the fact of the permanent richness of the drifts, and not only justify past expenditure, but a renewed outlay of credit and capital. The suspension of engineering work gave Mr. Carr an opportunity to visit San Francisco on general business of the mine, which could not, however, prevent him from arranging further combinations with capital. His two daughters accompanied him. It offered an admirable opportunity for a shopping expedition, a change of scene, and a peaceful solution of their perplexing and anomalous social relations with Devil's Ford. In the first flush of gratitude to their father for this opportune holiday, something of harmony had been restored to the family circle that had of late been shaken by discord.

But their sanguine hopes of enjoyment were not entirely fulfilled. Both Jessie and Christie were obliged to confess to a certain disappointment in the aspect of the civilization they were now reentering. They at first attributed it to the change in their own habits during the last three months, and their having become barbarous and countrified in their seclusion. Certainly in the matter of dress they were behind the fashions as revealed in Montgomery Street. But when the brief solace afforded them by the modiste and dressmaker was past, there seemed little else to be gained. They missed at first, I fear, the chivalrous and loyal devotion that had only amused them at Devil's Ford, and were the more inclined, I think, to distrust the conscious and more civilized gallantry of the better dressed and more carefully presented men they met. For it must be admitted that, for obvious reasons, their criticisms were at first confined to the sex they had been most in contact with. They could not help noticing that the men were more eager, annoyingly feverish, and self-asserting in their superior elegance and external show than their old associates were in their frank, unrestrained habits. It seemed to them that the five millionaires of Devil's Ford, in their radical simplicity and thoroughness, were perhaps nearer the type of true gentlemanhood than these citizens who imitated a civilization they were unable yet to reach.

The women simply frightened them, as being, even more than the men, demonstrative and excessive in their fine looks, their fine dresses, their extravagant demand for excitement. In less than a week they found themselves regretting— not the new villa on the slope of Devil's Ford, which even in its own bizarre fashion was exceeded by the barbarous ostentation of the villas and private houses around them— but the double cabin under the trees, which now seemed to them almost aristocratic in its grave simplicity and abstention. In the mysterious forests of masts that thronged the city's quays they recalled the straight shafts of the pines on Devil's slopes, only to miss the sedate repose and infinite calm that used to environ them. In the feverish, pulsating life of the young metropolis they often stopped oppressed, giddy, and choking; the roar of the streets and thoroughfares was meaningless to them, except to revive strange memories of the deep, unvarying monotone of the evening wind over their humbler roof on the Sierran hillside. Civic bred and nurtured as they were, the recurrence of these sensations perplexed and alarmed them.

"It seems so perfectly ridiculous," said Jessie, "for us to feel as out of place here as that Pike County servant girl in Sacramento who had never seen a steamboat before; do you know, I quite had a turn the other day at seeing a man on the Stockton wharf in a red shirt, with a rifle on his shoulder."

"And you wanted to go and speak to him?" said Christie, with a sad smile.

"No, that's just it; I felt awfully hurt and injured that he did not come up and speak to ME! I wonder if we got any fever or that sort of thing up there; it makes one quite superstitious."

Christie did not reply; more than once before she had felt that inexplicable misgiving. It had sometimes seemed to her that she had never been quite herself since that memorable night when she had slipped out of their sleeping-cabin, and stood alone in the gracious and commanding presence of the woods and hills. In the solitude of night, with the hum of the great city rising below her—at times even in theatres or crowded assemblies of men and women—she forgot herself, and again stood in the weird brilliancy of that moonlight night in mute worship at the foot of that slowly-rising mystic altar of piled terraces, hanging forests, and lifted plateaus that climbed forever to the lonely skies. Again she felt before her the expanding and opening arms of the protecting woods. Had they really closed upon her in some pantheistic embrace that made her a part of them? Had she been baptized in that moonlight as a child of the great forest? It was easy to believe in the myths of the poets of an idyllic life under those trees, where, free from conventional restrictions, one loved and was loved. If she, with her own worldly experience, could think of this now, why might not George Kearney have thought? . . . She stopped, and found herself blushing even in the darkness. As the thought and blush were the usual sequel of her reflections, it is to be feared that they may have been at times the impelling cause.

Mr. Carr, however, made up for his daughters' want of sympathy with metropolitan life. To their astonishment, he not only plunged into the fashionable gayeties and amusements of the town, but in dress and manner assumed the role of a leader of society. The invariable answer to their half-humorous comment was the necessities of the mine, and the policy of frequenting the company of capitalists, to enlist their support and confidence. There was something in this so unlike their father, that what at any other time they would have hailed as a relief to his habitual abstraction now half alarmed them. Yet he was not dissipated—he did not drink nor gamble. There certainly did not seem any harm in his frequenting the society of ladies, with a gallantry that appeared to be forced and a pleasure that to their critical eyes was certainly apocryphal. He did not drag his daughters into the mixed society of that period; he did not press upon them the company of those he most frequented, and whose accepted position in that little world of fashion was considered equal to their own. When Jessie strongly objected to the pronounced manners of a certain widow, whose actual present wealth and pecuniary influence condoned for a more uncertain prehistoric past, Mr. Carr did not urge a further acquaintance. "As long as you're not thinking of marrying again, papa," Jessie had said finally, "I don't see the necessity of our knowing her." "But suppose I were," had replied Mr. Carr with affected humor. "Then you certainly wouldn't care for any one like her," his daughter had responded triumphantly. Mr. Carr smiled, and dropped the subject, but it is probable that his daughters' want of sympathy with his acquaintances did not in the least interfere with his social prestige. A gentleman in all his relations and under all circumstances, even his cold scientific abstraction was provocative; rich men envied his lofty ignorance of the smaller details of money-making, even while they mistrusted his judgment. A man still well preserved, and free from weakening vices, he was a dangerous rival to younger and faster San Francisco, in the eyes of the sex, who knew how to value a repose they did not themselves possess.

Suddenly Mr. Carr announced his intention of proceeding to Sacramento, on further business of the mine, leaving his two daughters in the family of a wealthy friend until he should return for them. He opposed their ready suggestion to return to Devil's Ford with a new and unnecessary inflexibility: he even met their compromise to accompany him to Sacramento with equal decision.

"You will be only in my way," he said curtly. "Enjoy yourselves here while you can."

Thus left to themselves, they tried to accept his advice. Possibly some slight reaction to their previous disappointment may have already set in; perhaps they felt any distraction to be a relief to their anxiety about their father. They went out more; they frequented concerts and parties; they accepted, with their host and his family, an invitation to one of those opulent and barbaric entertainments with which a noted San Francisco millionaire distracted his rare moments of reflection in his gorgeous palace on the hills. Here they could at least be once more in the country they loved, albeit of a milder and less heroic type, and a little degraded by the overlapping tinsel and scattered spangles of the palace.

It was a three days' fete; the style and choice of amusements left to the guests, and an equal and active participation by no means necessary or indispensable. Consequently, when Christie and Jessie Carr proposed a ride through the adjacent canyon on the second morning, they had no difficulty in finding horses in the well-furnished stables of their opulent entertainers, nor cavaliers among the other guests, who were too happy to find favor in the eyes of the two pretty girls who were supposed to be abnormally fastidious and refined. Christie's escort was a good-natured young banker, shrewd enough to avoid demonstrative attentions, and lucky enough to interest her during the ride with his clear and half-humorous reflections on some of the business speculations of the day. If his ideas were occasionally too clever, and not always consistent with a high sense of honor, she was none the less interested to know the ethics of that world of speculation into which her father had plunged, and the more convinced, with mingled sense of pride and anxiety, that his still dominant gentlemanhood would prevent his coping with it on equal terms. Nor could she help contrasting the conversation of the sharp-witted man at her side with what she still remembered of the vague, touching, boyish enthusiasm of the millionaires of Devil's Ford. Had her escort guessed the result of this contrast, he would hardly have been as gratified as he was with the grave attention of her beautiful eyes.

The fascination of a gracious day and the leafy solitude of the canyon led them to prolong their ride beyond the proposed limit, and it became necessary towards sunset for them to seek some shorter cut home.

"There's a vaquero in yonder field," said Christie's escort, who was riding with her a little in advance of the others, "and those fellows know every trail that a horse can follow. I'll ride on, intercept him, and try my Spanish on him. If I miss him, as he's galloping on, you might try your hand on him yourself. He'll understand your eyes, Miss Carr, in any language."

As he dashed away, to cover his first audacity of compliment, Christie lifted the eyes thus apostrophized to the opposite field. The vaquero, who was chasing some cattle, was evidently too preoccupied to heed the shouts of her companion, and wheeling round suddenly to intercept one of the deviating fugitives, permitted Christie's escort to dash past him before that gentleman could rein in his excited steed. This brought the vaquero directly in her path. Perceiving her, he threw his horse back on its haunches, to prevent a collision. Christie rode up to him, suddenly uttered a cry, and halted. For before her, sunburnt in cheek and throat, darker in the free growth of moustache and curling hair, clad in the coarse, picturesque finery of his class, undisguised only in his boyish beauty, sat George Kearney.

The blood, that had forsaken her astonished face, rushed as quickly back. His eyes, which had suddenly sparkled with an electrical glow, sank before hers. His hand dropped, and his cheek flushed with a dark embarrassment.

"You here, Mr. Kearney? How strange!—but how glad I am to meet you again!"

She tried to smile; her voice trembled, and her little hand shook as she extended it to him.

He raised his dark eyes quickly, and impulsively urged his horse to her side. But, as if suddenly awakening to the reality of the situation, he glanced at her hurriedly, down at his barbaric finery, and threw a searching look towards her escort.

In an instant Christie saw the infelicity of her position, and its dangers. The words of Whiskey Dick, "He wouldn't stand that," flashed across her mind. There was no time to lose. The banker had already gained control over his horse, and was approaching them, all unconscious of the fixed stare with which George was regarding him. Christie hastily

Bret Harte

seized the hand which he had allowed to fall at his side, and said quickly:—

"Will you ride with mc a little way, Mr. Kearney?"

He turned the same searching look upon her. She met it clearly and steadily; he even thought reproachfully.

"Do!" she said hurriedly. "I ask it as a favor. I want to speak to you. Jessie and I are here alone. Father is away. YOU are one of our oldest friends."

He hesitated. She turned to the astonished young banker, who rode up.

"I have just met an old friend. Will you please ride back as quickly as you can, and tell Jessie that Mr. Kearney is here, and ask her to join us?"

She watched her dazed escort, still speechless from the spectacle of the fastidious Miss Carr tete-a-tete with a common Mexican vaquero, gallop off in the direction of the canyon, and then turned to George.

"Now take me home, the shortest way, as quick as you can."

"Home?" echoed George.

"I mean to Mr. Prince's house. Quick! before they can come up to us."

He mechanically put spurs to his horse; she followed. They presently struck into a trail that soon diverged again into a disused logging track through the woods.

"This is the short cut to Prince's, by two miles," he said, as they entered the woods.

As they were still galloping, without exchanging a word, Christie began to slacken her speed; George did the same. They were safe from intrusion at the present, even if the others had found the short cut. Christie, bold and self-reliant a moment ago, suddenly found herself growing weak and embarrassed. What had she done?

She checked her horse suddenly.

"Perhaps we had better wait for them," she said timidly.

George had not raised his eyes to hers.

"You said you wanted to hurry home," he replied gently, passing his hand along his mustang's velvety neck, "and—and you had something to say to me."

"Certainly," she answered, with a faint laugh. "I'm so astonished at meeting you here. I'm quite bewildered. You are living here; you have forsaken us to buy a ranche?" she continued, looking at him attentively.

His brow colored slightly.

"No, I'm living here, but I have bought no ranche. I'm only a hired man on somebody else's ranche, to look after the cattle."

He saw her beautiful eyes fill with astonishment and—something else. His brow cleared; he went on, with his old boyish laugh:

"No, Miss Carr. The fact is, I'm dead broke. I've lost everything since I saw you last. But as I know how to ride, and I'm not afraid of work, I manage to keep along."

"You have lost money in—in the mines?" said Christie suddenly.

"No"—he replied quickly, evading her eyes. "My brother has my interest, you know. I've been foolish on my own account solely. You know I'm rather inclined to that sort of thing. But as long as my folly don't affect others, I can stand it."

"But it may affect others—and THEY may not think of it as folly—" She stopped short, confused by his brightening color and eyes. "I mean—Oh, Mr. Kearney, I want you to be frank with me. I know nothing of business, but I know there has been trouble about the mine at Devil's Ford. Tell me honestly, has my father anything to do with it? If I thought that through any imprudence of his, you had suffered—if I believed that you could trace any misfortune of yours to him—to US—I should never forgive myself"—she stopped and flashed a single look at him—"I should never forgive YOU for abandoning us."

The look of pain which had at first shown itself in his face, which never concealed anything, passed, and a quick smile followed her feminine anticlimax.

"Miss Carr," he said, with boyish eagerness, "if any man suggested to me that your father wasn't the brightest and best of his kind—too wise and clever for the fools about him to understand—I'd—I'd shoot him."

Confused by his ready and gracious disclaimer of what she had NOT intended to say, there was nothing left for her but to rush upon what she really intended to say, with what she felt was shameful precipitation.

"One word more, Mr. Kearney," she began, looking down, but feeling the color come to her face as she spoke. "When you spoke to me the day you left, you must have thought me hard and cruel. When I tell you that I thought you were alluding to Jessie and some feeling you had for her—"

"For Jessie!" echoed George.

"You will understand that—that—"

"That what?" said George, drawing nearer to her.

"That I was only speaking as she might have spoken had you talked to her of me," added Christie hurriedly, slightly backing her horse away from him.

But this was not so easy, as George was the better rider, and by an imperceptible movement of his wrist and foot had glued his horse to her side. "He will go now," she had thought, but he didn't.

"We must ride on," she suggested faintly.

"No," he said with a sudden dropping of his boyish manner and a slight lifting of his head. "We must ride together no further, Miss Carr. I must go back to the work I am hired to do, and you must go on with your party, whom I hear coming. But when we part here you must bid me good-by— not as Jessie's sister—but as Christie—the one—the only woman that I love, or that I ever have loved."

He held out his hand. With the recollection of their previous parting, she tremblingly advanced her own. He took it, but did not raise it to his lips. And it was she who found herself half confusedly retaining his hand in hers, until she dropped it with a blush.

"Then is this the reason you give for deserting us as you have deserted Devil's Ford?" she said coldly.

He lifted his eyes to her with a strange smile, and said, "Yes," wheeled his horse, and disappeared in the forest.

He had left her thus abruptly once before, kissed, blushing, and indignant. He was leaving her now, unkissed, but white and indignant. Yet she was so self-possessed when the party joined her, that the singular rencontre and her explanation of the stranger's sudden departure excited no further comment. Only Jessie managed to whisper in her ear,—

"I hope you are satisfied now that it wasn't me he meant?"

"Not at all," said Christie coldly.

CHAPTER VII

A few days after the girls had returned to San Francisco, they received a letter from their father. His business, he wrote, would detain him in Sacramento some days longer. There was no reason why they should return to Devil's Ford in the heat of the summer; their host had written to beg him to allow them a more extended visit, and, if they were enjoying themselves, he thought it would be well not to disoblige an old friend. He had heard they had a pleasant visit to Mr. Prince's place, and that a certain young banker had been very attentive to Christie.

"Do you know what all this means, dear?" asked Jessie, who had been watching her sister with an unusually grave face.

Christie whose thoughts had wandered from the letter, replied carelessly,—

"I suppose it means that we are to wait here until father sends for us."

"It means a good deal more. It means that papa has had another reverse; it means that the assay has turned out badly for the mine—that the further they go from the flat the worse it gets—that all the gold they will probably ever see at Devil's Ford is what they have already found or will find on

Bret Harte

the flat; it means that all Devil's Ford is only a 'pocket,' and not a 'lead.'" She stopped, with unexpected tears in her eyes.

"Who told you this?" asked Christie breathlessly.

"Fairfax—Mr. Munroe," stammered her sister, "writes to me as if we already knew it—tells me not to be alarmed, that it isn't so bad—and all that."

"How long has this happened, Jessie?" said Christie, taking her hand, with a white but calm face.

"Nearly ever since we've been here, I suppose. It must be so, for he says poor papa is still hopeful of doing something yet."

"And Mr. Munroe writes to you?" said Christie abstractedly.

"Of course," said Jessie quickly. "He feels interested in—us."

"Nobody tells ME anything," said Christie.

"Didn't—"

"No," said Christie bitterly.

"What on earth DID you talk about? But people don't confide in you because they're afraid of you. You're so—"

"So what?"

"So gently patronizing, and so 'I-don't-suppose-you-can-help-it, poor-thing,' in your general style," said Jessie, kissing her. "There! I only wish I was like you. What do you say if we write to father that we'll go back to Devil's Ford? Mr. Munroe thinks we will be of service there just now. If the men are dissatisfied, and think we're spending money—"

"I'm afraid Mr. Munroe is hardly a disinterested adviser. At least, I don't think it would look quite decent for you to fly back without your father, at his suggestion," said Christie coldly. "He is not the only partner. We are spending no money. Besides, we have engaged to go to Mr. Prince's again next week."

"As you like, dear," said Jessie, turning away to hide a faint smile.

Nevertheless, when they returned from their visit to Mr. Prince's, and one or two uneventful rides, Christie looked grave. It was only a few days later that Jessie burst upon her one morning.

"You were saying that nobody ever tells you anything. Well, here's your chance. Whiskey Dick is below."

"Whiskey Dick?" repeated Christie. "What does he want?"

"YOU, love. Who else? You know he always scorns me as not being high-toned and elegant enough for his social confidences. He asked for you only."

With an uneasy sense of some impending revelation, Christie descended to the drawing-room. As she opened the door, a strong flavor of that toilet soap and eau de Cologne with which Whiskey Dick was in the habit of gracefully effacing the traces of dissipation made known his presence. In spite of a new suit of clothes, whose pristine folds refused to adapt themselves entirely to the contour of his figure, he was somewhat subdued by the unexpected elegance of the drawing-room of Christie's host. But a glance at Christie's sad but gracious face quickly reassured him. Taking from his hat a three-cornered parcel, he unfolded a handsome saffrona rose, which he gravely presented to her. Having thus reestablished his position, he sank elegantly into a tete-a-tete ottoman. Finding the position inconvenient to face Christie, who had seated herself on a chair, he transferred himself to the other side of the ottoman, and addressed her over its back as from a pulpit.

"Is this really a fortunate accident, Mr. Hall, or did you try to find us?" said Christie pleasantly.

"Partly promiskuss, and partly coincident, Miss Christie, one up and t'other down," said Dick lightly. "Work being slack at present at Devil's Ford, I reck'ned I'd take a pasear down to 'Frisco, and dip into the vortex o' fash'nable society and out again." He lightly waved a new handkerchief to illustrate his swallow-like intrusion. "This yer minglin' with the bo-tong is apt to be wearisome, ez you and me knows, unless combined with experience and judgment. So when them boys up there allows that there's a little too much fash'nable society and San Francisco capital and high-falutin' about the future goin' on fer square surface mining, I sez, 'Look yere, gentlemen,' sez I, 'you don't see the pint. The pint is to get the pop'lar eye fixed, so to speak, on Devil's Ford. When a fash'nable star rises above the 'Frisco horizon—like Miss Carr—and, so to speak, dazzles the gineral eye, people want to know who she is. And when people say that's the accomplished daughter o' the accomplished superintendent of the Devil's Ford claim—otherwise known as the Star-eyed Goddess o' Devil's Ford—every eye is fixed on the mine, and Capital, so to speak, tumbles to her.' And when they sez that the old man—excuse my freedom, but that's the way the boys talk of your father, meaning no harm—the old man, instead o' trying to corral rich widders—grass or otherwise—to spend their money on the big works for the gold that ain't there yet—should stay in Devil's Ford and put all his sabe and genius into grindin' out the little gold that is there, I sez to them that it ain't your father's style. 'His style,' sez I, 'ez to go in and build them works.' When they're done he turns round to Capital, and sez he—'Look yer,' sez he, 'thar's all the works you want, first quality—cost a million; thar's all the water you want, onlimited—cost another million; thar's all the pay gravel you want in and outer the ground—call it two millions more. Now my time's too vally'ble; my professhun's too high-toned to WORK mines. I MAKE 'em. Hand me over a check for ten millions and call it square, and work it for yourself.' So Capital hands over the money and waltzes down to run the mine, and you original locators walks round with yer hands in yer pockets a-top of your six million profit, and you let's Capital take the work and the responsibility."

Preposterous as this seemed from the lips of Whiskey Dick, Christie had a haunting suspicion that it was not greatly unlike the theories expounded by the clever young banker who had been her escort. She did not interrupt his flow of reminiscent criticism; when he paused for breath, she said, quietly:

"I met Mr. George Kearney the other day in the country."

Whiskey Dick stopped awkwardly, glanced hurriedly at Christie, and coughed behind his handkerchief.

"Mr. Kearney—eh—er—certengly—yes—er—met him, you say. Was he—er—er—well?"

"In health, yes; but otherwise he has lost everything," said Christie, fixing her eyes on the embarrassed Dick.

"Yes—er—in course—in course—" continued Dick, nerv-ously glancing round the apartment as if endeavoring to find an opening to some less abrupt statement of the fact.

"And actually reduced to take some menial employment," added Christie, still regarding Dick with her clear glance.

"That's it—that's just it," said Dick, beaming as he suddenly found his delicate and confidential opportunity. "That's it, Miss Christie; that's just what I was sayin' to the boys. 'Ez it the square thing,' sez I, 'jest because George hez happened to hypothecate every dollar he has, or expects to hev, to put into them works, only to please Mr. Carr, and just because he don't want to distress that intelligent gentleman by letting him see he's dead broke—for him to go and demean himself and Devil's Ford by rushing away and hiring out as a Mexican vaquero on Mexican wages? Look,' sez I, 'at the disgrace he brings upon a high-toned, fash'nable girl, at whose side he's walked and danced, and passed rings, and sentiments, and bokays in the changes o' the cotillion and the mizzourka. And wot,' sez I, 'if some day, prancing along in a fash'nable cavalcade, she all of a suddents comes across him drivin' a Mexican steer?' That's what I said to the boys. And so you met him, Miss Christie, as usual," continued Dick, endeavoring under the appearance of a large social experience to conceal an eager anxiety to know the details—"so you met him; and, in course, you didn't let on yer knew him, so to speak, nat'rally, or p'raps you kinder like asked him to fix your saddle-girth, and give him a five-dollar piece—eh?"

Christie, who had risen and gone to the window, suddenly turned a very pale face and shining eyes on Dick.

"Mr. Hall," she said, with a faint attempt at a smile, "we are old friends, and I feel I can ask you a favor. You once before acted as our escort—it was for a short but a happy time—will you accept a larger trust? My father is busy in Sacramento for the mine: will you, without saying anything to anybody, take Jessie and me back at once to Devil's Ford?"

"Will I? Miss Christie," said Dick, choking between an intense gratification and a desire to keep back its vulgar exhibition, "I shall be proud!"

"When I say keep it a secret"—she hesitated—"I don't mean that I object to your letting Mr. Kearney, if you happen to know where he is, understand that we are going back to Devil's Ford."

"Cert'nly—nat'rally," said Dick, waving his hand gracefully; "sorter drop him a line, saying that bizness of a social and delicate nature—being the escort of Miss Christie and Jessie Carr to Devil's Ford—prevents my having the pleasure of calling."

"That will do very well, Mr. Hall," said Christie, faintly smiling through her moist eyelashes. "Then will you go at once and secure tickets for to-night's boat, and bring them here? Jessie and I will arrange everything else."

"Cert'nly," said Dick impulsively, and preparing to take a graceful leave.

"We'll be impatient until you return with the tickets," said Christie graciously.

Dick shook hands gravely, got as far as the door, and paused.

"You think it better to take the tickets now?" he said dubiously.

"By all means," said Christie impetuously. "I've set my heart on going to-night—and unless you secure berths early—"

"In course—in course," interrupted Dick nervously. "But—"

"But what?" said Christie impatiently.

Dick hesitated, shut the door carefully, and, looking round the room, lightly shook out his handkerchief, apparently flicked away an embarrassing suggestion, and said, with a little laugh:

"It's ridiklous, perfectly ridiklous, Miss Christie; but not bein' in the habit of carryin' ready money, and havin' omitted to cash a draft on Wells, Fargo & Co.—"

"Of course," said Christie rapidly. "How forgetful I am! Pray forgive me, Mr. Hall. I didn't think. I'll run up and get it from our host; he will be glad to be our banker."

"One moment, Miss Christie," said Dick lightly, as his thumb and finger relaxed in his waistcoat pocket over the only piece of money in the world that had remained to him after his extravagant purchase of Christie's saffrona rose, "one moment: in this yer monetary transaction, if you like, you are at liberty to use MY name."

CHAPTER VIII

As Christie and Jessie Carr looked from the windows of the coach, whose dust-clogged wheels were slowly dragging them, as if reluctant, nearer the last stage of their journey to Devil's Ford, they were conscious of a change in the landscape, which they could not entirely charge upon their changed feelings. The few bared open spaces on the upland, the long stretch of rocky ridge near the summit, so vivid and so velvety during their first journey, were now burnt and yellow; even the brief openings in the forest were seared as if by a hot iron in the scorching rays of a half year's sun. The pastoral slopes of the valley below were cloaked in lustre-leather: the rare watercourses along the road had faded from the waiting eye and ear; it seemed as if the long and dry summer had even invaded the close-set ranks of pines, and had blown a simoom breath through the densest woods, leaving its charred red ashes on every leaf and spray along the tunnelled shade. As they leaned out of the window and inhaled the half-dead spices of the evergreens, they seemed to have entered the atmosphere of some exhausted passion— of some fierce excitement that was even now slowly burning itself out.

It was a relief at last to see the straggling houses of Devil's Ford far below come once more into view, as they rounded the shoulder of Devil's Spur and began the long descent. But

Bret Harte

as they entered the town a change more ominous and startling than the desiccation of the landscape forced itself upon them. The town was still there, but where were the inhabitants? Four months ago they had left the straggling street thronged with busy citizens—groups at every corner, and a chaos of merchandise and traders in the open plaza or square beside the Presbyterian church. Now all was changed. Only a few wayfarers lifted their heads lazily as the coach rattled by, crossing the deserted square littered with empty boxes, and gliding past empty cabins or vacant shop windows, from which not only familiar faces, but even the window sashes themselves, were gone. The great unfinished serpent-like flume, crossing the river on gigantic trestles, had advanced as far as the town, stooping over it like some enormous reptile that had sucked its life blood and was gorged with its prey.

Whiskey Dick, who had left the stage on the summit to avail himself of a shorter foot trail to the house, that would give him half an hour's grace to make preparations, met them at the stage office with a buggy. A glance at the young girls, perhaps, convinced him that the graces of elegant worldly conversation were out of place with the revelation he read on their faces. Perhaps, he, too, was a trifle indisposed. The short journey to the house was made in profound silence.

The villa had been repainted and decorated, and it looked fresher, and even, to their preoccupied minds, appeared more attractive than ever. Thoughtful hands had taken care of the vines and rose-bushes on the trellises; water—that precious element in Devil's Ford—had not been spared in keeping green through the long drought the plants which the girls had so tenderly nurtured. It was the one oasis in which the summer still lingered; and yet a singular sense of loss came over the girls as they once more crossed its threshold. It seemed no longer their own.

"Ef I was you, Miss Christie, I'd keep close to the house for a day or two, until—until—things is settled," said Dick; "there's a heap o' tramps and sich cattle trapsin' round. P'raps you wouldn't feel so lonesome if you was nearer town—for instance, 'bout wher' you useter live."

"In the dear old cabin," said Christie quickly; "I remember it; I wish we were there now."

"Do you really? Do you?" said Whiskey Dick, with suddenly twinkling eyes. "That's like you to say it. That's what I allus said," continued Dick, addressing space generally; "if there's any one ez knows how to come square down to the bottom rock without flinchin', it's your high-toned, fash'nable gals. But I must meander back to town, and let the boys know you're in possession, safe and sound. It's right mean that Fairfax and Mattingly had to go down to Lagrange on some low business yesterday, but they'll be back to-morrow. So long."

Left alone, the girls began to realize their strange position. They had conceived no settled plan. The night they left San Francisco they had written an earnest letter to their father, telling him that on learning the truth about the reverses of Devil's Ford, they thought it their duty to return and share them with others, without obliging him to prefer the request, and with as little worry to him as possible. He would find them ready to share his trials, and in what must be the scene of their work hereafter.

"It will bring father back," said Christie; "he won't leave us here alone; and then together we must come to some understanding with him—with THEM—for somehow I feel as if this house belonged to us no longer."

Her surmise was not far wrong. When Mr. Carr arrived

hurriedly from Sacramento the next evening, he found the house deserted. His daughters were gone; there were indications that they had arrived, and, for some reason, suddenly departed. The vague fear that had haunted his guilty soul after receiving their letter, and during his breathless journey, now seemed to be realized. He was turning from the empty house, whose reproachful solitude frightened him, when he was confronted on the threshold by the figure of Fairfax Munroe.

"I came to the stage office to meet you," he said; "you must have left the stage at the summit."

"I did," said Carr angrily. "I was anxious to meet my daughters quickly, to know the reason of their foolish alarm, and to know also who had been frightening them. Where are they?"

"They are safe in the old cabin beyond, that has been put up ready to receive them again," said Fairfax quietly.

"But what is the meaning of this? Why are they not here?" demanded Carr, hiding his agitation in a burst of querulous rage.

"Do YOU ask, Mr. Carr?" said Fairfax sadly. "Did you expect them to remain here until the sheriff took possession? No one knows better than yourself that the money advanced you on the deeds of this homestead has never been repaid."

Carr staggered, but recovered himself with feeble violence.

"Since you know so much of my affairs, how do you know that this claim will ever be pressed for payment? How do you know it is not the advance of a—a—friend?"

"Because I have seen the woman who advanced it," said

Fairfax hopelessly. "She was here to look at the property before your daughters came."

"Well?" said Carr nervously.

"Well! You force me to tell you something I should like to forget. You force me to anticipate a disclosure I expected to make to you only when I came to ask permission to woo your daughter Jessie; and when I tell you what it is, you will understand that I have no right to criticise your conduct. I am only explaining my own."

"Go on," said Carr impatiently.

"When I first came to this country, there was a woman I loved passionately. She treated me as women of her kind only treat men like me; she ruined me, and left me. That was four years ago. I love your daughter, Mr. Carr, but she has never heard it from my lips. I would not woo her until I had told you all. I have tried to do it ere this, and failed. Perhaps I should not now, but—"

"But what?" said Carr furiously; "speak out!"

"But this. Look!" said Fairfax, producing from his pocket the packet of letters Jessie had found; "perhaps you know the handwriting?"

"What do you mean?" gasped Carr.

"That woman—my mistress—is the woman who advanced you money, and who claims this house."

The interview, and whatever came of it, remained a secret with the two men. When Mr. Carr accepted the hospitality of the old cabin again, it was understood that he had sacrificed the new house and its furniture to some of the more pressing debts of the mine, and the act went far to restore his waning popularity. But a more genuine feeling of relief was experienced by Devil's Ford when it was rumored that Fairfax Munroe had asked for the hand of Jessie Carr, and that some promise contingent upon the equitable adjustment of the affairs of the mine had been given by Mr. Carr. To the superstitious mind of Devil's Ford and its few remaining locators, this new partnership seemed to promise that unity of interest and stability of fortune that Devil's Ford had lacked. But nothing could be done until the rainy season had fairly set in; until the long-looked-for element that was to magically separate the gold from the dross in those dull mounds of dust and gravel had come of its own free will, and in its own appointed channels, independent of the feeble auxiliaries that had hopelessly riven the rocks on the hillside, or hung incomplete and unfinished in lofty scaffoldings above the settlement.

The rainy season came early. At first in gathered mists on the higher peaks that were lifted in the morning sun only to show a fresher field of dazzling white below; in white clouds that at first seemed to be mere drifts blown across from those fresh snowfields, and obscuring the clear blue above; in far-off murmurs in the hollow hills and gulches; in nearer tinkling melody and baby prattling in the leaves. It came with bright flashes of sunlight by day, with deep, monotonous shadow at night; with the onset of heavy winds, the roar of turbulent woods, the tumultuous tossing of leafy arms, and with what seemed the silent dissolution of the whole landscape in days of steady and uninterrupted downfall. It came extravagantly, for every canyon had grown into a torrent, every gulch a waterspout, every watercourse a river, and all pouring into the North Fork, that, rushing past the settlement, seemed to threaten it with lifted crest and flying mane. It came dangerously, for one night the river, leaping the feeble barrier of Devil's Ford, swept away houses and banks, scattered with unconscious irony the laboriously collected heaps of gravel left for hydraulic machinery, and spread out a vast and silent lake across the submerged flat.

In the hurry and confusion of that night the girls had thrown open their cabin to the escaping miners, who hurried along the slope that was now the bank of the river. Suddenly Christie felt her arm grasped, and she was half-led, half-dragged, into the inner room. Her father stood before her.

"Where is George Kearney?" he asked tremulously.

"George Kearney!" echoed Christie, for a moment believing the excitement had turned her father's brain. "You know he is not here; he is in San Francisco."

"He is here—I tell you," said Carr impatiently; "he has been here ever since the high water, trying to save the flume and reservoir."

"George—here!" Christie could only gasp.

"Yes! He passed here a few moments ago, to see if you were all safe, and he has gone on towards the flume. But what he is trying to do is madness. If you see him, implore him to do no more. Let him abandon the accursed flume to its fate. It has worked already too much woe upon us all; why should it carry his brave and youthful soul down with it?"

The words were still ringing in her ears, when he suddenly passed away, with the hurrying crowd. Scarcely knowing what she did, she ran out, vaguely intent only on one thought, seeking only the one face, lately so dear in recollection that she felt she would die if she never saw it again. Perplexed by confused voices in the woods, she lost track of the crowd, until the voices suddenly were raised in one loud outcry, followed by the crashing of timber, the splashing of water, a silence, and then a dull, continuous roar. She ran vaguely on in the direction of the reservoir, with her father's injunction still in her mind, until a terrible idea displaced it, and she turned at right angles suddenly, and ran towards the slope leading down to the submerged flat. She had barely left the shelter of the trees behind her before the roar of water seemed to rise at her very feet. She stopped, dazed, bewildered, and horror-stricken, on the edge of the slope. It was the slope no longer, but the bank of the river itself!

Even in the gray light of early morning, and with inexperienced eyes, she saw all too clearly now. The trestle-work had given way; the curving mile of flume, fallen into the stream, and, crushed and dammed against the opposite shore, had absolutely turned the whole river through the half-finished ditch and partly excavated mine in its way, a few rods further on to join the old familiar channel. The bank of the river was changed; the flat had become an island, between which and the slope where she stood the North Fork was rolling its resistless yellow torrent. As she gazed spellbound, a portion of the slope beneath her suddenly seemed to sink and crumble, and was swallowed up in the rushing stream. She heard a cry of warning behind her, but, rooted to the spot by a fearful fascination, she heeded it not.

Again there was a sudden disruption, and another part of the slope sank to rise no more; but this time she felt herself seized by the waist and dragged back. It was her father standing by her side.

He was flushed and excited, gazing at the water with a strange exultation.

"Do you see it? Do you know what has happened?" he

asked quickly.

"The flume has fallen and turned the river," said Christie hurriedly. "But—have you seen him—is he safe?"

"He—who?" he answered vacantly.

"George Kearney!"

"He is safe," he said impatiently. "But, do you see, Christie? Do you know what this means?"

He pointed with his tremulous hand to the stream before them.

"It means we are ruined," said Christie coldly.

"Nothing of the kind! It means that the river is doing the work of the flume. It is sluicing off the gravel, deepening the ditch, and altering the slope which was the old bend of the river. It will do in ten minutes the work that would take us a year. If we can stop it in time, or control it, we are safe; but if we can not, it will carry away the bed and deposit with the rest, and we are ruined again."

With a gesture of impotent fury, he dashed away in the direction of an equally excited crowd, that on a point of the slope nearer the island were gesticulating and shouting to a second group of men, who on the opposite shore were clambering on over the choked debris of the flume that had dammed and diverted the current. It was evident that the same idea had occurred to them, and they were risking their lives in the attempt to set free the impediments. Shocked and indignant as Christie had been at the degrading absorption of material interests at such a moment, the element of danger lifted the labors of these men into heroism, and she began to feel a strange exultation as she watched them. Under the skilful blows of their axes, in a few moments the vast body of drift began to disintegrate, and then to swing round and move towards the old channel. A cheer went up, but as suddenly died away again. An overlapping fringe of wreckage had caught on the point of the island and arrested the whole mass.

The men, who had gained the shore with difficulty, looked back with a cry of despair. But the next moment from among them leaped a figure, alert, buoyant, invincible, and, axe in hand, once more essayed the passage. Springing from timber to timber, he at last reached the point of obstruction. A few strokes of the axe were sufficient to clear it; but at the first stroke it was apparent that the striker was also losing his hold upon the shore, and that he must inevitably be carried away with the tossing debris. But this consideration did not seem to affect him; the last blow was struck, and as the freed timbers rolled on, over and over, he boldly plunged into the flood. Christie gave a little cry—her heart had bounded with him; it seemed as if his plunge had splashed the water in her eyes. He did not come to the surface until he had passed the point below where her father stood, and then struggling feebly, as if stunned or disabled by a blow. It seemed to her that he was trying to approach the side of the river where she was. Would he do it? Could she help him? She was alone; he was hidden from the view of the men on the point, and no succor could come from them. There was a fringe of alder nearly opposite their cabin that almost overhung the stream. She ran to it, clutched it with a frantic hand, and, leaning over the boiling water, uttered for the first time his name:

"George!"

As if called to the surface by the magic of her voice, he rose a few yards from her in mid-current, and turned his fading eyes towards the bank. In another moment he would have been swept beyond her reach, but with a supreme effort he turned on one side; the current, striking him sideways, threw him towards the bank, and she caught him by his sleeve. For an instant it seemed as if she would be dragged down with him. For one dangerous moment she did not care, and almost yielded to the spell; but as the rush of water pressed him against the bank, she recovered herself, and managed to lift him beyond its reach. And then she sat down, half-fainting, with his white face and damp curls upon her breast.

"George, darling, speak to me! Only one word! Tell me, have I saved you?"

His eyes opened. A faint twinkle of the old days came to them—a boyish smile played upon his lips.

"For yourself—or Jessie?"

She looked around her with a little frightened air. They were alone. There was but one way of sealing those mischievous lips, and she found it!

"That's what I allus said, gentlemen," lazily remarked Whiskey Dick, a few weeks later, leaning back against the bar, with his glass in his hand. "'George,' sez I, 'it ain't what you SAY to a fash'nable, high-toned young lady; it's what you DOES ez makes or breaks you.' And that's what I sez gin'rally o' things in the Ford. It ain't what Carr and you boys allows to do; it's the gin'ral average o' things ez IS done that gives tone to the hull, and hez brought this yer new luck to you all!"

Bret Harte

ABOUT THE AUTHOR

Francis Bret Harte (August 25, 1836–May 6, 1902) was an American author and poet, best remembered for his accounts of pioneering life in California.

Born in Albany, New York, Harte moved to California in 1853, later working there in a number of capacities, including miner, teacher, messenger, and journalist. He spent part of his life in the northern California coast town now known as Arcata, at the time it was just a mining camp on Humboldt Bay.

His first literary efforts, including poetry and prose, appeared in The Californian, an early literary journal edited by Charles Henry Webb. In 1868 he became editor of The Overland Monthly, another new literary magazine, but this one more in tune with the pioneering spirit of excitement in California. His story, "The Luck of Roaring Camp," appeared in the magazine's second edition, propelling Harte to nationwide fame.

As an established literary figure, he was appointed to the position of United States Consul in the town of Krefeld, Germany in 1878 and Glasgow in 1880. In 1885 he settled in London. During the thirty years he spent in Europe, he never abandoned writing, and maintained a prodigious output of stories that retained the freshness of his earlier work. He died in England in 1902.

Choose from Thousands of 1stWorldLibrary Classics By

A. M. Barnard	Booth Tarkington	Edward Everett Hale
Ada Leverson	Boyd Cable	Edward J. O'Biren
Adolphus William Ward	Bram Stoker	Edward S. Ellis
Aesop	C. Collodi	Edwin L. Arnold
Agatha Christie	C. E. Orr	Eleanor Atkins
Alexander Aaronsohn	C. M. Ingleby	Eleanor Hallowell Abbott
Alexander Kielland	Carolyn Wells	Eliot Gregory
Alexandre Dumas	Catherine Parr Traill	Elizabeth Gaskell
Alfred Gatty	Charles A. Eastman	Elizabeth McCracken
Alfred Ollivant	Charles Amory Beach	Elizabeth Von Arnim
Alice Duer Miller	Charles Dickens	Ellem Key
Alice Turner Curtis	Charles Dudley Warner	Emerson Hough
Alice Dunbar	Charles Farrar Browne	Emilie F. Carlen
Allen Chapman	Charles Ives	Emily Bronte
Alleyne Ireland	Charles Kingsley	Emily Dickinson
Ambrose Bierce	Charles Klein	Enid Bagnold
Amelia E. Barr	Charles Hanson Towne	Enilor Macartney Lane
Amory H. Bradford	Charles Lathrop Pack	Erasmus W. Jones
Andrew Lang	Charles Romyn Dake	Ernie Howard Pie
Andrew McFarland Davis	Charles Whibley	Ethel May Dell
Andy Adams	Charles Willing Beale	Ethel Turner
Angela Brazil	Charlotte M. Braeme	Ethel Watts Mumford
Anna Alice Chapin	Charlotte M. Yonge	Eugene Sue
Anna Sewell	Charlotte Perkins Stetson	Eugenie Foa
Annie Besant	Clair W. Hayes	Eugene Wood
Annie Hamilton Donnell	Clarence Day Jr.	Eustace Hale Ball
Annie Payson Call	Clarence E. Mulford	Evelyn Everett-green
Annie Roe Carr	Clemence Housman	Everard Cotes
Annonaymous	Confucius	F. H. Cheley
Anton Chekhov	Coningsby Dawson	F. J. Cross
Archibald Lee Fletcher	Cornelis DeWitt Wilcox	F. Marion Crawford
Arnold Bennett	Cyril Burleigh	Fannie E. Newberry
Arthur C. Benson	D. H. Lawrence	Federick Austin Ogg
Arthur Conan Doyle	Daniel Defoe	Ferdinand Ossendowski
Arthur M. Winfield	David Garnett	Fergus Hume
Arthur Ransome	Dinah Craik	Florence A. Kilpatrick
Arthur Schnitzler	Don Carlos Janes	Fremont B. Deering
Arthur Train	Donald Keyhoe	Francis Bacon
Atticus	Dorothy Kilner	Francis Darwin
B.H. Baden-Powell	Dougan Clark	Frances Hodgson Burnett
B. M. Bower	Douglas Fairbanks	Frances Parkinson Keyes
B. C. Chatterjee	E. Nesbit	Frank Gee Patchin
Baroness Emmuska Orczy	E. P. Roe	Frank Harris
Baroness Orczy	E. Phillips Oppenheim	Frank Jewett Mather
Basil King	E. S. Brooks	Frank L. Packard
Bayard Taylor	Earl Barnes	Frank V. Webster
Ben Macomber	Edgar Rice Burroughs	Frederic Stewart Isham
Bertha Muzzy Bower	Edith Van Dyne	Frederick Trevor Hill
Bjornstjerne Bjornson	Edith Wharton	Frederick Winslow Taylor

Friedrich Kerst
Friedrich Nietzsche
Fyodor Dostoyevsky
G.A. Henty
G.K. Chesterton
Gabrielle E. Jackson
Garrett P. Serviss
Gaston Leroux
George A. Warren
George Ade
Geroge Bernard Shaw
George Cary Eggleston
George Durston
George Ebers
George Eliot
George Gissing
George MacDonald
George Meredith
George Orwell
George Sylvester Viereck
George Tucker
George W. Cable
George Wharton James
Gertrude Atherton
Gordon Casserly
Grace E. King
Grace Gallatin
Grace Greenwood
Grant Allen
Guillermo A. Sherwell
Gulielma Zollinger
Gustav Flaubert
H. A. Cody
H. B. Irving
H.C. Bailey
H. G. Wells
H. H. Munro
H. Irving Hancock
H. R. Naylor
H. Rider Haggard
H. W. C. Davis
Haldeman Julius
Hall Caine
Hamilton Wright Mabie
Hans Christian Andersen
Harold Avery
Harold McGrath
Harriet Beecher Stowe
Harry Castlemon
Harry Coghill
Harry Houidini

Hayden Carruth
Helent Hunt Jackson
Helen Nicolay
Hendrik Conscience
Hendy David Thoreau
Henri Barbusse
Henrik Ibsen
Henry Adams
Henry Ford
Henry Frost
Henry James
Henry Jones Ford
Henry Seton Merriman
Henry W Longfellow
Herbert A. Giles
Herbert Carter
Herbert N. Casson
Herman Hesse
Hildegard G. Frey
Homer
Honore De Balzac
Horace B. Day
Horace Walpole
Horatio Alger Jr.
Howard Pyle
Howard R. Garis
Hugh Lofting
Hugh Walpole
Humphry Ward
Ian Maclaren
Inez Haynes Gillmore
Irving Bacheller
Isabel Cecilia Williams
Isabel Hornibrook
Israel Abrahams
Ivan Turgenev
J.G.Austin
J. Henri Fabre
J. M. Barrie
J. M. Walsh
J. Macdonald Oxley
J. R. Miller
J. S. Fletcher
J. S. Knowles
J. Storer Clouston
J. W. Duffield
Jack London
Jacob Abbott
James Allen
James Andrews
James Baldwin

James Branch Cabell
James DeMille
James Joyce
James Lane Allen
James Lane Allen
James Oliver Curwood
James Oppenheim
James Otis
James R. Driscoll
Jane Abbott
Jane Austen
Jane L. Stewart
Janet Aldridge
Jens Peter Jacobsen
Jerome K. Jerome
Jessie Graham Flower
John Buchan
John Burroughs
John Cournos
John F. Kennedy
John Gay
John Glasworthy
John Habberton
John Joy Bell
John Kendrick Bangs
John Milton
John Philip Sousa
John Taintor Foote
Jonas Lauritz Idemil Lie
Jonathan Swift
Joseph A. Altsheler
Joseph Carey
Joseph Conrad
Joseph E. Badger Jr
Joseph Hergesheimer
Joseph Jacobs
Jules Vernes
Julian Hawthrone
Julie A Lippmann
Justin Huntly McCarthy
Kakuzo Okakura
Karle Wilson Baker
Kate Chopin
Kenneth Grahame
Kenneth McGaffey
Kate Langley Bosher
Kate Langley Bosher
Katherine Cecil Thurston
Katherine Stokes
L. A. Abbot
L. T. Meade

L. Frank Baum
Latta Griswold
Laura Dent Crane
Laura Lee Hope
Laurence Housman
Lawrence Beasley
Leo Tolstoy
Leonid Andreyev
Lewis Carroll
Lewis Sperry Chafer
Lilian Bell
Lloyd Osbourne
Louis Hughes
Louis Joseph Vance
Louis Tracy
Louisa May Alcott
Lucy Fitch Perkins
Lucy Maud Montgomery
Luther Benson
Lydia Miller Middleton
Lyndon Orr
M. Corvus
M. H. Adams
Margaret E. Sangster
Margret Howth
Margaret Vandercook
Margaret W. Hungerford
Margret Penrose
Maria Edgeworth
Maria Thompson Daviess
Mariano Azuela
Marion Polk Angellotti
Mark Overton
Mark Twain
Mary Austin
Mary Catherine Crowley
Mary Cole
Mary Hastings Bradley
Mary Roberts Rinehart
Mary Rowlandson
M. Wollstonecraft Shelley
Maud Lindsay
Max Beerbohm
Myra Kelly
Nathaniel Hawthrone
Nicolo Machiavelli
O. F. Walton
Oscar Wilde

Owen Johnson
P.G. Wodehouse
Paul and Mabel Thorne
Paul G. Tomlinson
Paul Severing
Percy Brebner
Percy Keese Fitzhugh
Peter B. Kyne
Plato
Quincy Allen
R. Derby Holmes
R. L. Stevenson
R. S. Ball
Rabindranath Tagore
Rahul Alvares
Ralph Bonehill
Ralph Henry Barbour
Ralph Victor
Ralph Waldo Emmerson
Rene Descartes
Ray Cummings
Rex Beach
Rex E. Beach
Richard Harding Davis
Richard Jefferies
Richard Le Gallienne
Robert Barr
Robert Frost
Robert Gordon Anderson
Robert L. Drake
Robert Lansing
Robert Lynd
Robert Michael Ballantyne
Robert W. Chambers
Rosa Nouchette Carey
Rudyard Kipling
Saint Augustine
Samuel B. Allison
Samuel Hopkins Adams
Sarah Bernhardt
Sarah C. Hallowell
Selma Lagerlof
Sherwood Anderson
Sigmund Freud
Standish O'Grady
Stanley Weyman
Stella Benson
Stella M. Francis

Stephen Crane
Stewart Edward White
Stijn Streuvels
Swami Abhedananda
Swami Parmananda
T. S. Ackland
T. S. Arthur
The Princess Der Ling
Thomas A. Janvier
Thomas A Kempis
Thomas Anderton
Thomas Bailey Aldrich
Thomas Bulfinch
Thomas De Quincey
Thomas Dixon
Thomas H. Huxley
Thomas Hardy
Thomas More
Thornton W. Burgess
U. S. Grant
Upton Sinclair
Valentine Williams
Various Authors
Vaughan Kester
Victor Appleton
Victor G. Durham
Victoria Cross
Virginia Woolf
Wadsworth Camp
Walter Camp
Walter Scott
Washington Irving
Wilbur Lawton
Wilkie Collins
Willa Cather
Willard F. Baker
William Dean Howells
William le Queux
W. Makepeace Thackeray
William W. Walter
William Shakespeare
Winston Churchill
Yei Theodora Ozaki
Yogi Ramacharaka
Young E. Allison
Zane Grey